Having spent a half century in the endeavor of defending the Christian faith, I can assure Christian leaders and parents that there is nothing more important to the future of the Christian Church than reaching this generation with the message of this book.

—DR. NORMAN L. GEISLER

Founder of the Evangelical Philosophical Society, International Society for Christian Apologetics and currently Distinguished Professor of Apologetics at Veritas Evangelical Seminary in Murrieta, CA

Dave Sterrett's book *Why Trust Jesus?* provides a true foundation of trust for both the Christian and the spiritual seeker. Dave tackles some of the toughest objections against trusting in Jesus in a way that is philosophically true and relationally relevant.

—JOSH MCDOWELL

Author of more than eighty books including *More Than a Carpenter* and *New Evidence That Demands a Verdict*

Why Trust Jesus? accentuates the necessity of loving God with both heart and mind by demonstrating the connection between knowledge and trust, emotion and intellect. Dave Sterrett offers a fresh approach to how we can know Jesus as a reliable, transparent, unconditionally loving friend, in whom we can place our complete trust.

—DR. JACK GRAHAM

Pastor, Prestonwood Baptist Church

In *Why Trust Jesus?* Dave Sterrett carefully and concisely responds to common questions in the hearts and minds of many of today's seekers of truth. He writes with authority as well as from personal experience, offering substantial historical references for anyone genuinely looking for answers that will lead to the peace that passes all understanding.

—ZIG ZIGLAR

Author/Motivational Teacher

This book by Dave Sterrett has offered the Christian community a rare gem— a type of homeland security for faith. With an unflinching eye and astute observations, this book will enable you to do more than defend the truth of the gospel . . . you will understand it.

—DR. ERGUN MEHMET CANER

President of Liberty Theological Seminary
Author of *Unveiling Islam: An Insider's Look at Muslim Life an*

One of the most endearing qualities of Christ was His ability to connect with the person on the street. The common people gladly listened to Him because He could frame eternal truth in terms that made sense to them. *Why Trust Jesus?* is in that same spiritual vein. Its value goes beyond the classroom and into the break room, and its place in this "bottom-line society" of ours is well-warranted.

—BOB COY
Senior Pastor, Calvary Chapel of Fort Lauderdale

Dave has an uncanny ability to take biblical truth and put it in a format that is easy enough to inspire those who have never been formally theologically trained, yet deep enough for someone seminary trained to discover new insights.

—CHRIS PLEKENPOL
I Am Second, Community Organizer

Dave Sterrett combines the mind of a classical philosopher with the heart of a passionate follower of Jesus Christ. Critical-thinking Christians and non-Christians alike will find *Why Trust Jesus?* to be a must read and will undoubtedly come away convinced.

—JONATHAN MERRITT
Spokesperson of the Southern Baptist Environment and Climate Initiative
Senior Editor of PastorsEdge.com

Dave Sterrett possesses a remarkable gift for creatively communicating God's truth. As a popular speaker and well-trained theologian, Dave passionately tackles some of the toughest spiritual questions being asked by our generation. His skill as a writer and teacher make him an important new voice in the field of Christian apologetics. Read this book—you'll never be the same!

—MARLA ALUPOAICEI
Author of *Your Intercultural Marriage: A Guide to a Healthy, Happy Relationship*

In a world that is consumed with self-sufficiency, "trying" has replaced "trusting" in the vocabulary of many believers. In this book, David Sterrett asks (and answers) some hard questions, all centered around trusting Christ's all-sufficiency. Read it and reap!

—O. S. HAWKINS
President and Chief Executive Officer GuideStone Financial Resources

When the question is asked today: "Whom do you trust?" I am afraid the answer from many in this generation would be, "No one . . . and why should I trust Jesus when there are other spiritual paths and when there is so much hate, hypocrisy, and death in the world?" In his book *Why Trust Jesus?*, Dave Sterrett answers these tough questions with compelling evidence from Scripture and philosophy.

—KERBY ANDERSON

National Director, Probe Ministries International

For a generation that does not trust Jesus, their parents, and many times not even themselves, this book on trust should speak to their hearts and show them how to put their trust in Jesus Christ for salvation and the Christian life.

—ELMER L. TOWNS

Cofounder, Liberty University, Dean, School of Religion

For such a young man, David Sterrett has had ministry experiences that few others have had. He has been exposed to many published authors in the field of apologetics, and has spent more than the normal amount of time with some of them, such as Josh McDowell and Norm Geisler. *Why Trust Jesus?* is the sort of brief, thoughtful, and directed response that we need to read.

—DR. GARY R. HABERMAS

Author of *The Case for the Resurrection of Jesus*

David Sterrett has written a seeker-sensitive book that will encourage those who have an interest in exploring and discovering truth. I also highly recommend this book as a tool for study. It will encourage those of us who know Christ to be better prepared as we engage our culture in conversation. May God use this book to advance His kingdom.

—STEVE WINGFIELD

Evangelist and President of the Steve Wingfield Evangelistic Association

Dave Sterrett answers the tough questions raised by the postmodern generation. Don't miss his insights to their thinking and his answers to their deepest issues.

—DR. ED HINDSON

Author of over fifteen books including *Courageous Faith*

We often feel compelled to approach the issues of faith in our day with defense or apologetic to challenge the thinking of an unbelieving world. Dave Sterrett takes this issue to a different level. He presents the attraction and appeal of the person of Jesus Christ and provides a credible basis for faith based upon His character. Dave strengthens his defense and simplifies his challenge by enabling the reader to see why it just makes sense to—trust Jesus.

—DR. DAVID H. MCKINLEY

Pastor of Warren Baptist Church, Augusta, Georgia

Rev. Sterrett has hit gold with his observations about trust. Simply put, trust is the currency of the kingdom. It is through trust that we enter the kingdom, live, and conduct our lives. Dave helps us work through the questions that must be addressed for us to be able to completely trust.

—DR. GERALD BROOKS

Pastor, Grace Outreach Center, Plano, TX, and author of *Ladder Focus.*

David Sterrett, in his book *Why Trust Jesus?*, has posed the question that so many people have asked throughout history. As you read this book, you will find that he has wrestled through the issues in order to give us practical, biblical answers, not just theological idioms.

—NAEEM FAZAL

Pastor of Mosaic Church, Charlotte

An honest look at **doubts, plans, hurts, desires, fears, questions,** and **pleasures**

Why Trust Jesus?

Dave **Sterrett**

Foreword by
Norman L. **Geisler**

MOODY PUBLISHERS

CHICAGO

Editor: Brandon O'Brien
Interior Design: Ragont Design
Cover Design and Image: Tan Nguyen
Author Photo: Katherine Robertson

Library of Congress Cataloging-in-Publication Data
Sterrett, Dave.
Why trust Jesus?: an honest look at doubts, plans, hurts, desires, fears,
questions, and pleasures / by Dave Sterrett.
    p. cm.
Includes bibliographical references.
ISBN 978-0-8024-8972-2
1. Trust in God. 2. Jesus Christ--Person and offices. I. Title.
BV4637.S735 2010
232'.8--dc22
                    2009040995

ISBN: 978-0-8024-8972-2

We hope you enjoy this book from Moody Publishers. Our goal is to provide high-quality, thought-provoking books and products that connect truth to your real needs and challenges. For more information on other books and products written and produced from a biblical perspective, go to www.moodypublishers.com or write to:

Moody Publishers
820 N. LaSalle Boulevard
Chicago, IL 60610

1 3 5 7 9 10 8 6 4 2

Printed in the United States of America

Contents

Foreword: Dr. Norman L. Geisler   10

Introduction: The Need for Transparent Trust   14

1. Why Should I Trust Jesus When There Are So
   Many Other Spiritual Paths?   24

2. Why Should I Trust Jesus When I'm Not Sure
   That a Supernatural God Is Real?   40

3. Why Should I Trust Jesus When I Have Been
   Let Down So Many Times?   56

4. Why Should I Trust Jesus When Life Seems to
   Be Going Just Fine without Him?   72

5. Why Should I Trust Jesus When All I Need to
   Do Is Trust Myself?   88

6. Why Should I Trust Jesus When There Is So Much
   Disagreement about the Identity of the "Real Jesus"?   102

7. Why Should I Trust Jesus More Than Any Other
   Spiritual Leader?   118

8. Why Should I Trust Jesus in the Midst of Suffering
   and Death?   134

9. Why Should I Trust Jesus When I Have Failed So
   Many Times?   150

Afterword: *Why I Trust Jesus* by Josh McDowell   161
Acknowledgments   165
Notes   167

To my parents, Clay and Teresa Sterrett
Your life encourages me to trust Jesus
and share His message of hope with others.

Foreword

Dr. Norman L. Geisler

Dr. Norman L. Geisler is founder of the
Evangelical Philosophical Society and the
International Society for Christian Apologet-
ics. He has authored hundreds of articles and
over seventy books, including *Baker Encyclo-
pedia of Christian Apologetics*. He is currently
Distinguished Professor of Apologetics at
Veritas Evangelical Seminary in Murrieta,
California (www.VeritasSeminary.com).

In the past several years, many people have had their trust shaken to the core. Some have lost their trust in personal safety in the midst of terrorism, school shootings, and war. Others have been rattled by hypocrisy in politics and even religion. New spirituality and new perspectives on Jesus are emerging. We are all looking to trust someone who is reliable and transparent, even in life's toughest moments.

This book addresses these tough issues and more, and will help people see the credibility of their Christian faith and its relevance to real life situations. It is born out of a solid training in apologetics and many years of successful ministry to youth by a leader in one of the top churches in America. Surveys show that approximately three out of four of young adults from good evangelical churches walk away from their faith while in college. This book is uniquely geared to help stop the bleeding.

Dave Sterrett adeptly addresses questions that many of us have wrestled with, including:

- Why should I trust Jesus when there are so many other spiritual paths?
- Why should I trust Jesus when I'm not sure that a supernatural God is real?
- Why should I trust Jesus when there is so much disagreement about the identity of the "real Jesus"?
- Why should I trust Jesus in the midst of suffering and death?
- Why should I trust Jesus when life seems to be going just fine without Him?

And many more.

I cannot think of a time in the recent history of the church when a book like this was so important. If we don't stop the serious leak in the "good ship evangelicalism," it's going to sink. And it is not for lack of repairmen that it is sinking. Unfortunately, most churches do not know it is sinking. The few who do are not utilizing the materials available to reach our students and young adults. Our entertainment-oriented society has influenced our churches. What we really need is not entertainment, but equipping to help us become effective witnesses for Christ in a post-Christian culture that has subtly but effectively eroded the very basis for their Christian faith.

We must heed the words of Scripture to give a reason for our hope (1 Peter 3:15), to defend the gospel (Philippians 1:7), and contend for the faith (Jude 3). This book communicates the message in a way that is profound yet easy to understand. It's not too late to save this generation for Christ, but the church will not be able to do it without fully equipping this generation to withstand the relativism, pluralism, and naturalism in our culture, which is destroying the very underpinnings of the Christian faith. Having spent a half century in the endeavor of defending the Christian faith, I can assure Christian leaders and parents that nothing is more important to the future of the Christian church than reaching this generation with the message of this book.

The Need for
Transparent Trust

August 15, 1980
Staunton, Virginia

Teresa couldn't believe what Dr. Coleman was telling her. "You're in labor," he said.

"I can't be. I have two more months." Because of complications, the baby was going to be delivered via cesarean section. One nurse called Teresa's husband, Clay, and another rushed her to the nearby hospital. The unintended delivery process had begun.

"It's a boy," the doctor said. "He is in respiratory distress, and we need to transport him immediately to the newborn intensive care unit at the University of Virginia. Would you like to see him before we take him to Charlottesville?"

"Yes, I would." Teresa spoke softly .

Minutes later, she looked over the right side of her bed at her baby, who lay in an infant incubator with a breathing tube connected to his mouth. She wished somehow she could hold and comfort him as she gently stroked the outside of the incubator and whispered, "I love you."

In the following days, Teresa's husband, Clay, would travel an hour between the two hospitals to visit his newborn son and his wife. After a day or two, it looked like Teresa was going to be all right, but the doctors were not as optimistic about the baby's future and wouldn't make any promises. "It could go either way," the doctor told Clay. "Your child lacks the ability to ventilate adequately. He also has an infection that we need to determine how to treat. We're not sure of the implications, but his lungs are not functioning properly."

A couple of days later, three of Clay's friends from the Community Fellowship Church in Staunton stopped by to pray for the baby. As they got down on their knees and prayed fervently, they felt assured that God would protect the child and were able to *trust* in God for the child's well-being.

At the same time, Teresa was still in Staunton's hospital, about forty miles from her newborn. The nurses allowed her to walk down the hall for the first time. She strolled past the nursery, where she noticed several young, smiling mothers holding their infants. She began to pray quietly, "Lord, you know it's important for mothers to hold their babies, but mine is on the other side of the mountain. He's out of my care, and I don't even know if he's going to make it . . ."

Mysteriously, after praying a few moments, Teresa sensed a warm embrace, even though she didn't see anybody. Was it God? Even though she had a sincere faith in God, this was a strange experience. She sensed that God was letting her know that her baby was going to be healthy and live. It was as if God were saying, "I love you, and I'm with your child. Just as you feel My embrace, your child is experiencing the same thing. He's in My hands."

About a week and a half later, Teresa was able to take her healthy baby home from the UVA hospital. Born two months premature, I weighed five pounds, thirteen and one half ounces. One doctor estimated that if I would have stayed in my mother's womb the entire term, I might have weighed eleven pounds. Poor Mom. Looking back, I understand that my parents trusted in the sovereignty of God.

They didn't know the outcome, but they prayed and placed their trust in Him. Fortunately, God gave me life. But just because we trust Jesus doesn't mean that everything is going to turn out like we want. Sometimes our prayers remain unanswered, and we must trust that God understands things beyond our comprehension.

A couple of years ago, I was back in Staunton, Virginia, visiting my parents. They took me to the gravesite where their two baby girls are buried. The premature births of my sisters ended in death when my mom was about five months pregnant with each. During both pregnancies, my parents fervently prayed and trusted in Jesus for a successful outcome. Friends and family prayed and trusted, but the prayers went unanswered. Despite their severe disappointment and sadness, my parents continued to trust God. Yet, as I stood beside my parents at the little gravesite twenty-five years later, I detected the pain in my mother's heart was still present. I watched a tear roll down her face as my father put his arm around her to comfort her. Some pain is never entirely forgotten.

Sometimes, we struggle to trust Christ when things are not going well. Some people just want to give up. Other people wrestle with trusting God because things are going well. They become self-sufficient and depend on themselves rather than looking to God. The purpose of this book is to encourage you to trust Christ regardless of what you have been through or what you are experiencing right now.

I asked my parents, "Why did you still trust Jesus, even when your prayers went unanswered?" My mom responded by referring to the character and nature of God. She told me that God knows everything. His mind is infinite and understands things that we don't fully grasp. My dad quoted King David's words, "I would have despaired unless I had believed that I would see the goodness of the Lord in the land of the living."[1] In a fallen world, bad things can happen to all people, but in the midst of evil, we understand a transcendent source of goodness. My dad also said, "I rest in the sovereignty of God."

Some people who doubt God's existence might say these answers were good for my parents, but don't work for them. A lot of us, including me, struggle with trust because we think we are unique and that "nobody knows the trouble I've seen." Sometimes, after having these thoughts of pity regarding my personal struggles of trust, I meet someone or hear about something that I can't imagine experiencing.

SHATTERED TRUST

I heard about a college student, whom I will refer to as Ryan,[2] at Virginia Tech. He recalled that he was on his way to class near Norris Hall on April 16, 2007, when he saw the chaos. Ryan later recounted, "This teacher comes flying out of Norris; he's bleeding from his arm or his shoulder . . . all these students were coming out of Norris trying to take shelter in Randolph [Hall]. All these kids were freaked out."[3] Then came the announcement that would quickly circulate around the globe: "Thirty-two confirmed dead, and at least another twenty-one are wounded."

By noon, Virginia Tech President Charles Steger said at a news conference: "The University is shocked and horrified that this would befall our campus . . . I cannot begin to convey my own personal sense of loss over the senselessness of such an incomprehensible and heinous act." After that horrific incident, Ryan, his fellow students, and a host of other people not only suffered tremendous grief, but many seemed to be asking deeper questions: How could this happen? Why wasn't something done to prevent it? Who can we trust to protect us?

Most of us have seen our trust in personal safety erode as terrorists, snipers, and other attackers have harmed innocent people, such as on the campus of Virginia Tech. Our generation also has constantly faced the unpleasant realities of war and rumors of more war. Since 9/11, people of multiple faiths have believed that the end of the world may be near. Mahmoud Ahmadinejad, the president of Iran, is developing nuclear weapons and has said that he wants to wipe Israel off the face of the earth. The Middle East faces constant crisis and strives in vain for lasting peace.

In the last decade of my life, I have seen trust shaken at every level. In recent years, this uncertainty has become even more acute as many Americans have lost faith in the stock market and cannot depend on Social Security pensions. Some people have lost their homes, millions are still trying to get out of debt, and a number of economic indicators have revealed numbers at their lowest levels since the Great Depression. Confidence and approval ratings in some government leaders continue to plummet. Employees in prominent corporations have lost their trust in their job security and retirement savings as a number of business executives have been exposed in their greed and deceitfulness. Retirees have seen life savings evaporate overnight as the result of schemes and fraud on the part of trusted investment advisers. In addition, big-name athletes are charged with alleged acts of steroid abuse, assault, gambling, or other illegal activities. Lots of churchgoers have lost their trust in their religious leaders. Numerous priests have resigned because of sexual abuse. The big question in everyone's mind is, "Can we trust anyone anymore?"

Some of us who grew up in church have often heard the phrase, "Trust in Jesus," as a platitude, as if it were a magical phrase that would somehow instantly make everything better. Even worse, our pastors or parents might have used it as a cop-out to avoid providing real answers to our difficult questions.

Even though we claim to be Christ-followers, as time passes, many of us struggle with that same simple concept of trust. Trust is confidence; it is a conviction of the reliability of something or someone. As human beings, we have a longing in our souls to trust someone. Even though many of us have been hurt and misled by friends, family members, or leaders we once respected, we still have a craving—a deep desire for something that we can believe in, for someone in whom we can trust.

19

Trust can be broken relationally, emotionally, and intellectually. In the college classroom, a Christian student may encounter a distinguished professor who says it is intellectual suicide or a blind "leap of faith" to place our trust in a historical person named Jesus who lived two thousand years ago. For another student who has experienced twenty years of life with minimum difficulties, she finds out that two close friends are killed in a car wreck. Another young lady experiences a breakup from her Christian boyfriend that hurts her in a way that words cannot express. Others witness hypocrisy in the life of a pastor whom their family has known and trusted for years. For many, depression comes when one's Christian parents divorce, perhaps after years of apparently devoted marriage.

We all have different struggles: strained relationships, disappointments, hurts, broken hearts, or the untimely deaths of loved ones. Then we find ourselves in a place we never thought we would be in, as we wrestle with the issue of trust and even begin to question God (His existence or the authenticity and reliability of His Son, Jesus).

Carrie, a gifted Christian female student at Temple University, told me:

> I struggle with trust. I grew up in a Christian family in Pennsylvania, and I always saw my parents involved with church. They were good parents. Yet, during a time in my life when I needed my father the most, he left the family, and my parents got a divorce. I watched my mom go through crises of pain. I hurt when I saw my mom hurt. And I began to fill a void in my life by dating guy after guy, but they dishonored me. These were guys who were Christians, but they treated me with no dignity or respect. I struggle with whom I can trust.

How many of us struggled with our relationship with God when we were students? How many of us are like Carrie, suddenly thrown into a tailspin when something in which we trusted was torn right out from under us? How do we know that we can bring our broken hearts and shattered trust to Jesus, not to be disappointed yet again? How can we know that trusting Jesus is the *true* answer for every struggling person, regardless of race or background or circumstances?

The Battle for Trust

A newly married couple has just joined a church. They loved their pastor's teaching at their church in Colorado. Many of his sermons were on morality, integrity, love, and purity. Yet he got caught lying to them and was living a promiscuous and hypocritical lifestyle. This pastor could not be trusted. If he could not be trusted, then *why trust Jesus?*

A friend of mine, Abdoul Diallo, a former Muslim from West Africa, is now a Christian and a student at Harvard. After Abdoul's conversion to Christianity, he wanted to tell everybody about Jesus, including his brother, who was pursuing a PhD at the University of Cairo in Egypt. Abdoul persuaded his brother that the Quran was not true, and his brother went back to share the gospel with his fellow students and professors. Two days later, Abdoul's brother was found shot to death. Abdoul also recently lost his mother, who was murdered by his father when she took a stand for Abdoul's belief in Christ. Abdoul will testify that life still is not easy living in America. Living as a Christian has not been trouble-free for Abdoul. In fact, his faith has cost him the two people he loved most in this world. Now he is asking himself, *Why trust Jesus?*

At a prestigious university on the East Coast, a student is dealing with trust issues. His religion professor says that the Bible we read today is not historically reliable and lacks confidence in foundational doctrines of Christianity. This same religion professor studied Christianity at Wheaton College and Princeton Seminary but now considers himself an agnostic. The young believer is wondering if the church and his youth pastor deceived him by telling him that Jesus was the Son of God and that the Bible was historically reliable. He is confused about truth. He wants to know, *Why trust Jesus?*

A young single mother has been mistreated by men. Her father left her mother when she was ten, and the stepfather who followed sexually abused her. To make matters worse, her husband recently left her and her daughter for somebody else. She struggles with trusting men and is also asking, *Why trust Jesus?*

Whom Do We Trust?

We generally trust people who are:

- Truthful
- Reliable
- Transparent
- Authentic
- Loving
- Faithful
- Forgiving

Rarely does a person exhibit all these qualities, but one man in history certainly did. He was a sinless man, perfect in actions and attitude. Even the enemies of Jesus praised His character. Pilate said, "I find no fault in this man."[4] Yet despite the trustworthiness of Jesus in all facets of His life and character, many people have intellectual barriers as well as experiential doubts that keep them from trusting Jesus fully.

In this book, we'll examine some tough questions that can create roadblocks that keep us from trusting Jesus on our life's journey. This book will provide some real spiritual answers that give philosophical, historical, scientific, biblical, and relational evidence to trust in Jesus. The answers will serve as a strong foundation to trust

Jesus even when life gets difficult. People start doubting Christ because of relational difficulties, spiritual struggles and intellectual doubts. Others decide not to trust Christ because they believe they are managing life just fine without Him. They see other non-Christians who are successful in life and don't see the need to trust in Jesus. Nevertheless, in moments of fear, grief, difficulty, and disappointment, some of those people look once again for someone they can trust.

This generation isn't necessarily opposed to spirituality or to Jesus Himself, but perhaps they are like I was—longing for authentic, fulfilling relationships and true freedom. This book confidently shows that there is someone we can trust—His name is Jesus! He reveals His existence in reality through history. Through an encounter of His Holy Spirit, Christ invites you to know, trust, and follow Him. The Bible says He is "the Rock! His works are perfect, and all His ways are just; a God of faithfulness and without injustice, righteous and upright is He."[5]

Chapter One

. . . .

Why Should I Trust Jesus When There Are So Many Other Spiritual Paths?

> *"Stand at the crossroads and look; ask for the ancient paths, ask where the good way is, and walk in it, and you will find rest for your souls."*
>
> —Jeremiah 6:16

Oak Hill Academy, set in the heart of the beautiful Blue Ridge Mountains on the southwestern border of Virginia, is nationally known for being a basketball powerhouse. It has won national championships and produced all-Americans such as Carmelo Anthony. At the age of eighteen, I headed there for my last year of high school with the sole intention of playing basketball with the best and the brightest young stars. My coach, Steve Smith, was a four-time *USA Today* High School Coach of the Year. My team and I traveled to Los Angeles, Minneapolis, and Las Vegas, and competed in exciting matchups against some of the most talented teams across the country.

Little did I know that God was going to teach me greater lessons that year than those I learned on the basketball court (and on the bench, which I often kept warm!). While I had expected to battle rival teams on the basketball court, I had no idea that the biggest battle would be the one for my faith.

At this Christian boarding school, I was required to attend chapel during the week as well as church on Sunday morning. One day in chapel, the pastor prayed something like this: "Dear God, some of us call you Father or Jesus, some of us call you Allah, some of us call you other names, but we know that you are the same God of us all—a God of love." Throughout the year, the pastor continued to pray similar prayers.

Many people didn't think anything was wrong with praying such an "inclusive" prayer. In fact, I truly believe that my pastor had a genuine heart of love for the student body. He was attempting to welcome students with a diverse range of spiritual beliefs. Some of the students of other faiths included my Muslim friends from Egypt as well as my buddy from Senegal, with whom I normally ate lunch. But the implication of my pastor's prayers and teaching was an attack on the religious exclusivism to which I held (more on that below).

Even though I had some good friends at Oak Hill, I felt alone at times. My beliefs were not always popular on campus. Most of my peers and even some of my teachers considered me narrow-minded and judgmental for believing that Christianity is exclusively true. Although I lived far away from my family and church, I realized that my pastor's prayer was contrary to what the early historical church believed about Jesus Christ: "There is salvation in no one else, for there is no other name under heaven given to men by which we must be saved."[1] I knew that Jesus Himself claimed religious exclusivity when He said, "I am the way and the truth and the life. No one comes to the Father except through me."[2]

What I experienced as an eighteen-year-old at Oak Hill Academy is not unusual for many young Christians. In fact, today, if you claim that your religion is exclusively true, you are often regarded as an intolerant, narrow-minded, bigoted extremist. And many people don't know how to respond when their claims about Christ are attacked. As a result, they're walking away from *believing* and *trusting* the historic Christ of the Bible.

When my pastor prayed, "Dear God, some of us call you Father or Jesus, some of us call you Allah," etc., I did not know exactly what to do, but I knew I had to do something. I knew that his prayer was contrary to the Bible, so I started praying that God would use me to change the situation. I wanted to be spiritually prepared; I was not going to be popular claiming that Jesus Christ was "*the* way, *the* truth and *the* life."

As I continued to pray, I felt compelled to ask the pastor if he would allow me to preach for him some Sunday morning in church. Before this, I didn't have a strong desire to speak or teach, but I became convinced that the student body needed to hear the truth and love of Jesus Christ. To my surprise the pastor said, "Yes!"

I felt convinced that if someone discovered a cure for cancer, he should share that information with others to help those who are dying from cancer. As human beings we have something worse than cancer, called sin. We have proven ourselves to be selfish, prideful, and sometimes hateful. But God gave us the cure for sin through the person of Jesus Christ. Because of God's extravagant love, I was convinced that the student body needed to hear the truth about His love and mercy. So I called my dad, who is a minister, and asked him if he could help me prepare the outline of a message. I started preparing.

One day, as I was praying, I felt led by the Lord to go to talk to a particular student named Chase. I didn't know why God wanted me to go to Chase's room, but I thought that maybe God would use me to tell him about Jesus. So I showed up at his dorm and introduced myself. Chase recognized who I was. I guess I stood out on campus because I am six feet seven inches tall. As Chase and I talked, I mentioned something about spirituality to see how he would react. To my surprise, Chase told me that he was a Christian. We were both excited, because we didn't know many students who would talk openly about being a Christian. I suggested to Chase that we have a Bible study, and he agreed. However, we both had a lot of homework so we decided to meet another time.

As I made my way back to my dorm, I was overcome with a sense of urgency to do something. I felt that God was leading me to go back to Chase's dorm immediately and have a Bible study. I had no idea how to lead a Bible study, so I grabbed my sermon notes that I was working on and took them back to Chase's room. I said, "Chase, I know this seems weird, but I believe that God wants us to have a Bible study right now, even though we both have a lot of homework. I don't know how to lead a Bible study, but I am actually working on my first sermon and am a little nervous about public speaking, so I thought I could practice it for you. You could critique me, and then we could pray."

Chase said, "Go ahead; let's do it."

I asked Chase's roommate, Ethan, to join us, and even though it was a little awkward, I started preaching to the two of them. I gave a simple sermon, similar to the style of Billy Graham, on John 3:16 (NKJV): "For God so loved the world, that he gave his only begotten Son, that whoever believes in him should not perish but have everlasting life." At the end of my message, I practiced giving an invitation for anyone in the audience who wanted to accept Christ.

When I was finished, Ethan said, "That's really good. When you give that message at church, I am going to pray to receive Christ."

I looked at him, a little astonished, and said, "You can pray to *trust Jesus* as your Savior right now." I said a prayer out loud, and he repeated it as he prayed to trust Jesus.

As we finished praying, a couple of guys walked by the room. They seemed surprised to see me there. They asked what we were doing. I said, "Guys, we're having a Bible study. Come on in!" I gave the same message on John 3:16 to them, and when I was done, one of the guys said, "Dave, that makes sense. I need to believe in Jesus." Once again, I led this student in a simple prayer for him to trust in Christ. I told these guys to come back the next day and bring some friends. When I arrived the next day, there were several new people in the room, and as I practiced the same sermon, two more young men prayed to receive Christ.

I announced to the group that we needed to start a weekly Bible study and asked them to bring some more friends the next week.

That night, I set an important goal for myself: to personally tell every single student on that campus about Christ. On one occasion, I was having a conversation with a friend of mine in the library who was an outspoken lesbian. I shared with her about the love of God through Christ. She started weeping when I started telling her how much God loved her. I was a little shocked at the sight of her tears, because I didn't think I said anything offensive. She shared with me how much she was hurting on the inside and that she became convicted of her sin and wanted to receive the love of Christ.

The group grew, and people started coming who I didn't expect. A couple of my Muslim friends showed up, one guy who claimed to be a Satanist dropped by, and others who were agnostics and atheists attended, too. We had a question-and-answer time after each session, and some people started to ask tough questions. They asked about the truth of the Bible, about other religions, about salvation by grace (as opposed to salvation by works), and about religious exclusivity. These were hard questions, and I didn't have all of the answers.

Weeks later, I preached at the church, and people responded very positively to the good news of salvation through Jesus. Even the pastor was encouraging of my message. Doors started opening for me to speak at other small churches in the area, and people also started asking more questions about Christianity.

Again, I didn't know all of the answers. Even though it was exciting at times to see people become interested in Jesus, it was not always easy. In fact, sometimes it got downright discouraging, because some of the people that prayed to "trust Jesus" ended up walking away from Christianity and some people stopped coming to Bible study.

As I struggled with these disappointments, I was challenged to continue trusting Jesus. I faced some issues in my life. I knew that I had a relationship with Christ that was true regardless of what I was feeling, but I also knew that I needed to continue in my pursuit of knowing Him more deeply. Even though I didn't discover every answer, I developed a conviction that truth was absolute, regardless of what I felt. My assurance of absolute truth remained firm, even if some of my friends would judge me for not being a relativist or pluralist.

That year, my basketball team ended up winning the championship ring. We were declared national champions by ESPN and *USA Today*. But my greatest victory that year was the opportunity to share the reasons for trusting Jesus with others and to grow in that trust myself. God taught me so much about trust in the process. Almost a decade later, I'm still searching for answers to some questions, but fortunately, I've also discovered some profound spiritual truths.

My life's message to all people (which grew out of the trials that catapulted me into a search for truth) is simply this: God loves you. He loves you so much that He sent His Son to die for your sins, and He has given you a heart and mind to passionately follow Him. It *is* possible to know truth.

Life isn't always easy, and sometimes circumstances don't work out the way you think they should, but even in the midst of some uncertainties, you can be sure of certain truths. You can trust Jesus. He will reveal himself to you when you seek Him with all of your heart, soul, and mind. You can have this certainty in Christ, because God has first given us a sureness founded on the basis of the knowledge of reality.

FAITH UNDER FIRE?

Even though Christianity is spreading more rapidly worldwide than ever before, if a person living in the United States claims that Jesus Christ is exclusively the Truth, he or she will appear absurd to many. Born in India, Christian apologist Ravi Zacharias writes:

> We are living in a time when sensitivities are at the surface, often vented with cutting words. Philosophically, you can

believe anything, so long as you do not claim it to be true. Morally, you can practice anything, so long as you do not claim that it is a better way. Religiously, you can hold to anything, so long as you do not bring Jesus Christ into it.[3]

Zacharias continues, "If a spiritual idea is eastern, it is granted critical immunity; if western, it is thoroughly criticized. Thus, a journalist can walk into a church and mock its carryings on, but he or she dare not do the same if the ceremony is from the eastern fold. Such is the mood of the twentieth century."[4] In today's atmosphere of intolerance toward Christianity, followers of Christ must have the foundation of knowing the historical Jesus (who, by the way, was not Western, but Eastern). If we are ridiculed or even hated for our faith, we must have a base of knowledge that's unshakable. We will speak of the true Jesus in the chapters to come, but it is important that we have a foundational understanding that reality *is* indeed knowable. If truth is knowable, then our trust in truth has greater conviction.

Exclusivism isn't a popular word today. In our society, we face opposition when we claim that our religion of Christianity is absolutely true. Religious exclusivism teaches that one religion is exclusively true, as opposed to religious pluralism, which teaches that multiple religions, often contradicting religions, are equally true.

The Oprah Winfrey Show presents a good example of religious pluralism expressed today through popular media. Often on this show, a guest will talk about his or her experiences with spirituality or morality. Sometimes Oprah will ask the audience for their opinions about the topic. On one occasion, when a member of the audience responded by referencing a biblical example, Oprah respectfully said, "One of the mistakes that human beings make is believing that there is only one way to live, and we don't accept that there are diverse ways of being in the world."[5] She added, "There are many paths to what you call God. Her path may be something else, and when she gets there she may call it the Light."[6] When another audience member disagreed with Oprah and said that Jesus was the only way, Oprah responded by saying, "There can't possibly be one way. I can't get into a religious argument with you right now."

Religious pluralism claims to be open-minded, but is it really? When we stop and think about the claims of religious pluralism, we discover that this worldview doesn't accept any faith expression that is *not* pluralistic. Even though pluralism is touted at many universities as "open-mindedness," it's actually just another form of religious exclusivity. Why? Because it excludes anybody who doesn't believe it. Therefore, religious pluralism excludes the beliefs of hundreds of millions of Christians who claim that Jesus Christ is the only way for salvation.

Interestingly, it's not just Christianity that claims to be exclusively true. Muhammed, the founder of Islam, claimed Islam to be the true religion, and the teachers of Hinduism say *it* is the true religion. Then some Hindus decided to reject certain teachings of Hinduism, so they split off and started a new religion called Buddhism. Buddhism today includes hundreds of sects, each of which has its own set of spiritual beliefs. Religious pluralism rejects any of these religions that claim that their way is the *one* way that is true and correct. When you think about how many billions of people in the world follow these religions, you realize that most people are *not* true religious pluralists.

In addition to the fact that many are attacking our beliefs in the historical Christ and His claim to be the giver of salvation, many Americans are apathetic about or ignorant of spiritual things. Many of the people who are interested in spirituality are simply longing for a quick fix or an emotional experience. I heard a story in which someone was asked, "What is the greatest problem in our culture: ignorance or apathy?" To this, the person responded by saying, "I don't know, and I don't care!"

Consider the words of pop singer Britney Spears: "I think I'm more grounded, you know, and I know what I want out of life and

I'm, you know, my morals are really, you know, strong, and I have major beliefs about certain things, and I think that has helped me."[7] Her words echo the thoughts of many celebrities in our culture whose actions tell us that, "I really don't care about the most important things in life."

Many people continue to look to celebrities and Hollywood for guidance. J. P. Moreland, who holds a PhD in philosophy from the University of Southern California, summed up the recent spiritual thought of many in Western culture:

> Spirituality is in, but no one knows which form to embrace. Indeed, the very idea that one form may be better than another seems arrogant and intolerant. A flat stomach is of greater value than a mature character. The makeup man is more important than the speech writer. People listen, or pretend to listen, to what actors—actors—have to say! Western Civ had to go and, along with it, the possibility of getting a robust university education. Why? Because political correctness so rules our universities that they are now places of secular indoctrination, and one is hard-pressed to find serious classroom interaction from various perspectives on the crucial issues of our day.[8]

In our culture, why should we trust Jesus when people have so many other spiritual beliefs? In order for someone to have a reasonable trust in Jesus, he or she must have knowledge of the truth about His existence. Is it possible to trust someone you don't know? Well, yes, to some extent. When you vote for a political candidate, you may not know everything about him or her, but you vote for someone about whom you at least know certain things. You understand the underpinnings, the "heart," of what is important in that candidate's stand. The strongest trust is based on that about which one has knowledge.

Jesus calls us to a "trust" that is not antagonistic toward evidence and reason. Many Christians mistakenly believe that Jesus called His disciples to a "blind faith" or to a "leap of faith." Truthfully, He called them to a "trust" based on fact, evidence, and reason. This doesn't mean that God reveals all the answers immediately. Jesus called His disciples first *and then* spent three years with them, living out a life that they could observe and trust. However, the trust to which He calls us is not opposed to reason.

Let's look at the dialogue between Jesus and His disciples recorded by one of Jesus' closest disciples, John, right before Jesus is about to be turned over to the Roman soldiers to be put on trial, brutally beaten, mocked, and then executed. Jesus knows that He is about to die, and He treasures the time He has left with His disciples. The last words He speaks to them and for them are so vital. Jesus could have spoken about a number of other things, but He chose to talk to them about *trust*:

> "Do not let your hearts be troubled. Trust in God; trust also in me. In my Father's house are many rooms, if it were not so, I would have told you. I am going there to prepare a place for you. And if I go and prepare a place for you, I will come back and take you to be with me that you also may be where I am. You know the way to the place where I am going."
>
> Thomas said to him, "Lord, we don't know where you are going, so how can we know the way?"
>
> Jesus answered, "I am the way and the truth and the life. No one comes to the Father except through me. If you really knew me, you would know my Father as well. From now on, you do know him and have seen him."[9]

Thomas and Phillip are a bit skeptical by nature. Phillip, with grave doubts, asked for some evidence so that he could place his trust in Jesus and the Father. Jesus, rather than asking them to practice a "blind faith," always offers evidence that shows why they can trust Him. Let's continue in the passage in John:

Philip said, "Lord, show us the Father and that will be enough for us." Jesus answered: "Don't you know me, Philip? . . . Believe me when I say that I am in the Father and the Father is in me; or at least believe on the evidence of the miracles themselves."[10]

Jesus didn't say, "Just blindly trust what I am telling you." No! He gave evidence of His claims throughout the time He spent with the disciples by performing miracles before them. Jesus also predicted His supernatural physical resurrection a few verses later when he said, "Because I live, you also will live." Philip, though skeptical, also believed in Christ because of the testimony of the laws and prophets that spoke of the coming Messiah. We'll discuss these prophecies and the resurrection in further detail in the chapters to come. But for now, we want to emphasize that Jesus does not call us to blindly trust in Him. Rather, He tells us to trust something of which we have knowledge.

Some people may say, "Well, that might be true for you, but it's not true for me," because they believe that truth is not objective. This view is called *relativism,* which is similar to the religious pluralism that we discussed earlier. Relativism in regard to truth teaches that truth is not discovered by an individual or group of people, but is created or determined by the individual or group of people. This view may teach that the Bible is true for those who have faith or belief in it, but not necessarily true for those who do not have faith in it.

The foundation of trusting in Jesus is that He is true. But if absolute truth does not exist, then to say that "Jesus is the Truth" is a meaningless statement. Many definitions of truth fail, but a good definition of truth is "that which corresponds to reality"; simply put, truth is "telling it like it is." Paul Copan, in *True for You, But Not for Me,* lists several characteristics of truth:

- Something can be true even if no one knows it.
- Something can be true even if no one admits it.
- Something can be true even if no one agrees what it is.
- Something can be true even if no one follows it.
- Something can be true even if no one but God grasps it fully.[11]

Copan continues, "Although some states have given up trying to figure out whom to blame for car accidents, hence no-fault insurance, truth matters. And when the stakes are raised, when a child crossing the street is hit by a truck and killed, for example, finding the truth becomes essential. Serious circumstances remind us that the difficulty of finding truth is no excuse for not looking."[12]

We all insist on knowing the truth in our daily lives. We have expectations that the court will convict only the truly guilty. We expect to know the truth in our relationships. Most people never enter a relationship expecting their loved one to be untruthful or unfaithful. Even with simple daily tasks like going to the bank, we expect the banker to tell us the truth about our finances. We want the doctor to tell us the truth about our medical condition. When you need to use a public restroom, you expect the truth when you read the "men" or "women" sign.

In order for someone to trust Jesus, he must have knowledge that the claims of Jesus are true. Dr. R. C. Sproul notes:

> Trust is personal—it is a special part of any close human relationship. Trust is a by-product of truth, and personal relationships are built upon trust. I trust people who demonstrate that they are truthful. I do not trust people who show themselves to be habitual liars. A person who is trustworthy is a person who is truthful.[13]

Today, some people are attempting to deny absolute truth and the simple laws of logic. When this happens, a person often commits the fallacy of giving a *self-defeating statement*. A self-defeating statement is a statement that fails to meet its own standard. For example, if someone said, "I can't speak of word of English," in English, this would be a self-defeating statement. Why? Because he or she just spoke that sentence *in English*!

In the same way, if someone says, "There is no absolute truth!" you could respond by saying, "Is that absolutely true?" If so, the person has just contradicted himself or herself. If someone says, "You can't *know any truth* about God!" you could respond by saying, "How do you *know* that about God being unknowable?" That in itself is a "truth claim" that the person is professing to know. It's a self-defeating statement.

People attempt to violate the simple laws of logic at academic institutions, at work, in Hollywood, and in everyday life. Actress and singer Mandy Moore was once asked in an interview, "What's your biggest pet peeve now that you've been in the industry awhile?" Mandy responded by saying, "People who don't take others into consideration." She continued, "I don't like [people who] are intolerant—whether it be of race or religion or sexual preference. It really gets me going."[14]

If you had been there, you could have asked Ms. Moore, "Aren't you being *intolerant* of intolerant people?" It is true that tolerance can be a positive attribute at times, but it's equally true that people should be intolerant of some things. I am thankful that Abraham Lincoln was intolerant of slavery, Martin Luther King Jr. was intolerant of racism, that Billy Graham is intolerant of sin, and that Winston Churchill was intolerant of oppression. Isn't Mandy Moore being intolerant when she says, "I don't like (people who) are intolerant"? As we mentioned earlier, relativism (or the denial of absolutes, which is found in this new so-called tolerance) is not consistently open-minded. It violates the simple laws of logic.

When a person trusts in Christ, he or she must understand that Jesus is Truth. If Jesus Christ and His teachings are absolutely true, then anything opposed to Him is false. Truth is a cornerstone to authentic trust. When Christians stop believing in absolute truth, their worldviews, and eventually their lifestyles, will both be affected.

Research done by George Barna and Josh McDowell reports how one's beliefs affect one's behavior. Barna and McDowell discovered that if a person doesn't believe in absolute truth, he or she will be:

- 200% more likely to steal
- 200% more likely to watch a pornographic film
- 300% more likely to use illegal drugs
- 600% more likely to attempt suicide[15]

When people deny absolute truth, the foundations of their personal convictions are knocked off course, and the next thing to go off track is their behavior. It's critical that we *know truth* as a foundation of trusting Jesus. Unfortunately, most people in our culture do not believe in the importance of being grounded with a strong foundation of knowledge. Some people just want to have "blind faith" in Christ that only involves the heart and feelings while excluding the mind and reason. This is contrary to what Jesus Himself commanded. He wants us to offer Him our heart *and* our mind. Jesus said that the greatest commandment is to "Love the Lord your God, with all of your heart and with all of your soul, and with all of your *mind*."[16]

In the book of Isaiah, God says, "Come now, let us reason together."[17] God the Father also wants our minds and our hearts. In order for us to trust Him, we must involve both heart and intellect. Some of us don't like to study, because studying God's truth takes focus and discipline. However, such discipline ought to be part of the Christian life. Jesus said, "If anyone would come after me, he must deny himself and take up his cross and follow me."[18] Paul said, "Discipline yourself for the purpose of godliness."[19] This certainly includes mental discipline as well.

One of the reasons that you can trust Jesus is because He loves you so much that He has given you a mind that can embrace the truth about reality. The book of Psalms says, "Those who know your name trust in you, for you, Lord, have never forsaken those who seek you."[20] It's not a trusting in something that we don't know, but it's trusting in something we can know, even if our knowledge is limited.

We don't have to have all of the answers (in fact, we never will on this side of heaven), but God calls us to passionately pursue His truth. God says in the Bible, "You will seek Me and find Me when you search for Me with all of your heart."[21] Another verse says, "Some trust in chariots and some in horses, but we trust in the name of the Lord our God."[22] He assures us that He is worthy of our trust. Once we have a foundation of knowing truth, then we can pursue Him, and once we know Him, we trust what He tells us in His Word.

That's what happened to me when I was a senior in high school at Oak Hill Academy. I wasn't a skilled teacher or speaker. I didn't have the answers to every difficult theological question that the guys threw at me. But God allowed me to discover His truth step-by-step. I had made up my mind to pursue truth in the journey of trusting Jesus.

Although we all have a unique life journey, salvation is received through placing our faith in the sacrificial atonement of Christ alone. We discuss this more in future chapters, but we can acknowledge that one of the reasons we trust Christ is because the truth about spiritual beliefs is knowable. With certainty beyond a reasonable doubt, we can know and experience that truth. Because of this foundation, we will be able to trust Jesus, who reveals Himself to us in truth.

Chapter Two

Why Should I Trust Jesus When I'm Not Sure That a Supernatural God Is Real?

> *"There is no one we can more safely trust than God Himself in regard to the fact that it was He who made the world."*
>
> —St. Augustine

At age fifteen, a brilliant British student named Jack abandoned the Christian faith of his childhood and became an atheist. Several years earlier, Jack had experienced a traumatic event that most boys his age couldn't imagine: his mother had died of cancer. Because of that painful experience, Jack rejected his Christian upbringing and turned to other forms of spirituality, mythology, and the occult in search of answers.

As Jack grew older, he began to recognize the injustices of life. He felt, for example, that his elite preparatory school focused too much on social status. As a result, he left his school to study privately with his father's tutor, Mr. Kirkpatrick, who instilled in him a love of Greek literature and mythology and sharpened his proficiency in reasoning and debate. Jack eventually won a scholarship to attend Oxford and received the highest honors in Greek and Latin literature, philosophy, ancient history, and English.

As a young lecturer in his twenties, this self-proclaimed atheist became very angry at the fact that God did not exist. He quoted the ancient Epicurean philosopher Lucretius as having one of the strongest arguments for atheism:

"Had God designed the world, it would not be
A world so frail and faulty as we see."[1]

Because Jack was not sure that Jesus or God even existed, he didn't know how to trust Jesus. However, Jack's close friend, a Catholic, genuinely trusted Jesus and showed Jack that he cared about him. They met regularly at the pub to drink and discuss literature. When the topic of religion came up, Jack's friend (the author J.R.R. Tolkien) not only talked about God's existence but also gave sound arguments for why he trusted God. After listening to his friend and reading influential books by G. K. Chesterton and George MacDonald, Jack eventually chose to follow Christ. He said himself that he "came into Christianity kicking and screaming."

Jack, also known as C. S. Lewis, describes his conversion in his book *Surprised by Joy*:

You must picture me alone in that room in Magdalene, night after night, feeling, whenever my mind lifted even for a second from my work, the steady, unrelenting approach of Him whom I so earnestly desired not to meet. That which I greatly feared had at last come upon me. In the Trinity Term of 1929, I gave in, and admitted that God was God, and knelt and prayed: perhaps, that night, the most dejected reluctant convert in all England.[2]

In 1929, Jack encountered reasons to believe in God's existence. In 1931, he placed his trust in Jesus.

Like C. S. Lewis, some open-minded people struggle to know why to trust Jesus because they are not even sure that God and Jesus really exist. They may have suffered through painful circumstances that triggered doubts about God. Some students wrestle with trust because their atheist professors indoctrinate them with a version of naturalistic evolution that goes beyond observable science and pushes a philosophical agenda that denies the supernatural. Students who might be agnostic (not sure if God exists or not) are led to believe that God does not exist in reality, so miracles probably are impossible and the so-called miracles of Jesus are ridiculous to trust.

Some simply believe that one can have a vague faith in God, just like some children have faith in the existence of a benevolent Santa Claus or Easter Bunny. Others who admit the possibility of God's existence fail to acknowledge the logical connection that if God did one miracle in history (create the universe), then other miracles are at least *possible.* If God can create all of the oceans *out of nothing,* why shouldn't His Son, Jesus, have been able to turn water into wine? Surely it would have been no problem for God to part the Red Sea. For Jesus, walking on water or calming a storm with a single word would have been a cakewalk. If God is the author of all life, then it is not beyond the realm of reason that His Son could die and come back to life.

The skeptic philosopher David Hume (who, by the way, was skeptical of just about everything except for his own skepticism) indicated that a wise person should *never* believe in miracles because they are "rare events." Really? Haven't we reasonably believed in the factual nature of many other rare events, including:

1. The origin of the universe. (No matter what theory of creation a person believes, most would agree that the universe came into being as it presently exists, only *once!*)
2. Events in the history of mankind. (President Abraham Lincoln was killed only once; Microsoft software was invented by one man, Bill Gates; and the World Trade Center's Twin Towers were destroyed on one date, September 11, 2001.

These events happened one time in history, but we *believe* that they happened.)
3. Your own birth. (You were born only one time, yet you confidently believe that this rare event happened!)

Hume believed that it was unwise for someone to place his or her faith in rare events, yet he probably had faith in such "rare events" as his own birth! In the Bible, miracles were *supposed* to be rare events. When Jesus performed miracles, it was a sign that He was the Messiah. Miracles were an indication that He possessed the power and blessing of God the Father.

CAN WE KNOW THAT GOD EXISTS WITHOUT THE BIBLE OR OTHER SACRED WRITINGS?

Even though I love to share the beauty of Scripture with those who might not believe in its authority, I also believe we need to defend some of our beliefs about God using philosophy, history, and science in well-stated arguments.

Paul the apostle used this method when he had a conversation with the naturalistic Epicurean philosophers in Athens.[3] And Jesus talked about His Father's existence with illustrations of objects in creation. If a person does not believe that there is a God, then she won't believe or trust a Son of God (Jesus), nor will she believe or trust in a Word of God (the Bible). So, for the sake of the spiritual seeker, we must learn to articulate reasons for God's existence without primarily looking to the Scriptures.

In the early fifth century, a Christian leader named Augustine echoed Paul's words as he encouraged young preachers and teachers to defend the truth, using the tools of logic, language, and philosophy. He wrote, "Since rhetoric is used to give conviction to both truth and falsehood, who could dare to maintain that truth, which depends on us for its defense, should stand unarmed in the fight against falsehood?"[4] Centuries later, C. S. Lewis wrote, "To be ignorant and simple now—not to be able to meet the enemies on their own ground—would be to throw down our weapons, and to betray our uneducated brethren who have, under God, no defense but us against the intellectual attacks of the heathen. Good philosophy must exist, if for no other reason, because bad philosophy needs to be answered."[5]

REASONS TO TRUST THAT GOD EXISTS: GOD MUST BE THE DESIGNER OF THE UNIVERSE

The concept of intelligent design (ID) teaches that there is a design in the universe. The design may be observed in several areas such as the intricate astronomical evidence of the universe's origin or the detailed information discovered in DNA. Most proponents of ID believe that it is more probable that the universe was designed purposely by some form of intelligence than by pure chance or luck. Although proponents of ID do not necessarily believe that the universe was designed by God, it is true that many of them will acknowledge that only a being who is very powerful (like God) could design the universe. Even the famous atheist Richard Dawkins, who claims to be antagonistic toward the concept of an intelligent designer, in his interview with Ben Stein hinted at the possibility that *aliens* could have designed the world.[6]

Modern atheists will use arguments similar to the ancient philosopher Lucretius, who appeals to the imperfections of the world to disprove that God was the creator. But imperfect design still implies a designer. When atheists ask why an all-benevolent being would create a world with natural disasters, disease, and death, they are actually asking a theological question about the nature of God. The design argument doesn't defend the character of God's goodness or perfection. ID simply argues that empirical evidence in the universe suggests the existence of a designer.

In the 1997 movie *Contact*, based on the 1985 book by Carl Sagan, Ellie (played by Jodie Foster) monitors radio waves and signals from outer space, listening for an ordered, encrypted sequence among the static. She and her scientist colleagues eventually decipher a signal that is, as they describe it, "not local." As a result, they surmise that a complex, ordered pattern "can only come from an intelligent source."[7]

Let me share another analogy. Suppose you were to visit the Louvre Museum in Paris and found yourself gazing at one of the world's most popular paintings—the Mona Lisa. Would you conclude that this was just an accident from an explosion in a paint store? You are more likely to assume that the remarkable work was done by an accomplished painter (designer).

The argument from design was popularized by an Anglican theologian, William Paley, who published Natural Theology in 1802. Paley wrote, "In crossing a heath, suppose I pitched my foot against a stone, and were asked how the stone came to be there, I might possibly answer, for anything I knew to the contrary, it had lain there forever." Paley continued, "But suppose I found a watch upon the ground, I should hardly think of the answer I had given before."[8]

Paley was making the point that you don't have to be an expert in watches or even stones to understand that someone designed the watch. You may not know who exactly created the watch, but you know someone did.[9]

Some Darwinian naturalistic atheists will criticize this argument by showing its limitations in describing the nature of the intelligent designer. These same atheists often fail to admit the faith that is involved in some of the mysteries of evolution, too. Just as there some things that we do not understand about intelligent design, naturalistic scientists do not fully understand evolution. Once again, intelligent design does not attempt to describe all of the moral attributes of God (love, justice, mercy, etc.). It simply claims that it is more likely that the probability of fine-tuning points toward intelligence rather than accident or happenstance.

Astronomer Hugh Ross identifies hundreds of examples that suggest that the universe was precisely created and "tweaked" to support human life on Earth. For example, the size of our galaxy is perfect. If the Milky Way were larger, infusions of gas and stars would disturb the sun's orbit and cause too many galactic eruptions. If it were smaller, there would be an insufficient infusion of gas to sustain star formation.[10] Similarly, the oxygen and nitrogen quantity on Earth was just right for life. If there were more oxygen, plants and hydrocarbons would burn up too easily. If there was less oxygen, then advanced animals would have too little to breathe. Given these and hundreds of other examples of precise "fine-tuning" in the universe, it is *most* probable that an intelligent designer was involved in the creation of the universe.

Other aspects of the universe—like the structure and order of a person's DNA—also support the theory of intelligent design. Dr. Francis Collins is one of the leading DNA scientists in the world and head of the Human Genome Project. In his book, *The Language of God,* he also reveals that he is a man of unshakable faith in God and Scripture.[11]

Collins recalls an announcement about the Human Genome Project, in the year 2000, that appeared in virtually every major newspaper. He stood with then-president Bill Clinton and was joined by then–British prime minister Tony Blair by satellite. In the president's address, Clinton said, "Without a doubt, this is the most important, most wondrous map ever produced by humankind." Reflecting on Clinton's speech, Collins noted, "But the part of his speech that most attracted public attention jumped from the scientific perspective to the spiritual." Clinton had said, "Today, we are learning the language in which God created life. We are gaining ever more awe for the complexity, the beauty, and the wonder of God's most divine and sacred gift."[12]

Collins found Clinton's observation compelling. "Was I, a rigorously trained scientist," he asked, "taken aback at such a blatantly religious reference by the leader of the free world at a moment like this? No, not at all."[13] Francis Collins is one of many scientists who do not see a problem in believing that science points to God.

You do not have to be an expert in science or philosophy to see that the evidence of the design in the universe implies, beyond a reasonable doubt, an Intelligent Designer. For many years Antony Flew was known as one of the world's leading atheists. But Flew abandoned his atheism and accepted the existence of God because of the argument from design. Flew explained his new beliefs in an interview for *Philosophia Christi* with Gary Habermas: "[I] had to go where the evidence leads."

When we establish a personal relationship with God by trusting Christ, we do not receive all of the answers about God's nature immediately. Nevertheless, we can go wherever the evidence leads. Sometimes I wonder why atheists such as Richard Dawkins admit that aliens might have been involved in the creation of our world but get angry when someone suggests that the world's designer is God. Perhaps it's because if God exists, then there are moral implications for the way we live our lives and treat one another.

GOD MUST BE THE FIRST CAUSE OF THE UNIVERSE

A second case for God's existence is known as the "cosmological" argument. This line of reasoning asserts that God is the First Cause of the cosmos (or universe). Simply put, the argument develops like this:

1. Everything that had a beginning had a cause.
2. The universe had a beginning.
3. Therefore, the universe had a cause.

In science class you learned the principle of causality that says everything that begins needs a cause. Without this principle, science would be impossible. Even the great skeptic David Hume could not deny the law of causality. "I never asserted so absurd a proposition," he wrote, "as that something could arise without a cause."[14] Geisler and Turek comment on this law: "So if anyone ever tells you he doesn't believe in the Law of Causality, simply ask them, 'What *caused* you to come that conclusion?'[15]

The second premise says that *the universe had a beginning.* Although this may seem obvious now, at the start of the twentieth century, quite a few scientists believed that the universe was eternal with no beginning. In the last century, however, an abundance of scientific discoveries has affirmed that the universe must have had a beginning. In 1927, the influential cosmologist Edwin Hubble observed through his telescope, by means of the movements of distant galaxies and the wavelengths of their light, that the universe was expanding. Hubble's discovery has caused most astronomers to conclude that the universe had an absolute beginning, because they understand that if we were to hypothetically reverse the expansion, we would arrive at nothing—the point at which the expansion began. As physicist Stephen Hawking puts it, "Almost everyone now believes that the universe, and *time itself,* had a beginning at the Big Bang."[16]

Many scientists even identify the Big Bang with God's acts of creation as recorded in Genesis. Scientist Gerald Schroeder, who earned his PhD in physics from MIT, says, "Creation, in biblical language, refers to the Eternal's introduction into the universe of something from nothing. It is an instantaneous act. Genesis 1:1 is teaching that in the beginning, in an instantaneous flash now known as the big bang, God created from absolute nothing the raw materials of the universe."[17] Similarly, the agnostic astrophysicist Robert Jastrow wrote in *God and the Astronomers,* "Now we see how the astronomical evidence leads to a biblical view of the origin of the world. The details differ, but the essential elements and the astronomical and biblical accounts of Genesis are the same; the chain of events leading to man commenced suddenly and sharply at a definite moment in time, in a flash of light and energy."[18]

If it is true that the universe had a definite beginning, it takes only a small step of faith into the light to believe that *someone* caused the universe to exist. But it takes a huge step of faith into the dark to believe that *no one* caused the universe to exist. If someone did create the universe, then that Being must have been all-powerful. Although this argument does not tell us anything about this Being's character, it does suggest the existence of the Being philosophers and theologians refer to as *the Almighty.*

GOD MUST BE THE MORAL LAWGIVER

I recently had a conversation with a lady at Starbucks who found out I was a Bible teacher at a Christian academy affiliated with a conservative evangelical church. She asked me, "So what are your thoughts on homosexuality?"

I have been in similar ethical conversations before. Often when a person asks me a question like this, he or she wants me to say quickly whether or not I think homosexual behavior is wrong. Then the person (who might even be a homosexual) might say something like, "That's why I don't go to church—because you Christians are judgmental and hate gays." So, because I knew where the conversation was headed by the tone of her voice, I decided not to quote a Bible verse or give her a quick answer. Instead, I replied, "That's an interesting question. Why do you ask?"

And just as I expected, she responded by saying how judgmental it is for certain Christians to say homosexuality is wrong. Instead of disagreeing with her, I asked her another question. "Do you think that anything is wrong?"

She looked at me a little stunned and said, "Of course."

"Do you think that there is anything *wrong* with any specific sexual acts, such as rape, child abuse, other forms of pedophilia, and bestiality?"

With a disgusted look on her face, she said, "Well, of course those things are wrong."

I paused a minute to let that soak in and then asked her, "What's your *basis* for saying it's wrong?" She responded that pedophilia imposes itself on others and hurts innocent children. I pressed her.

"But you still haven't told me *why* it is wrong."

A little confused, she looked to me as if she wanted an explanation. I explained to her that there must be an objective moral standard that goes beyond the rapist and victim, a standard that transcends society, and determines what is right and what is wrong. After she admitted the possibility of objective moral laws, it makes most sense that God is the moral lawgiver. If a person's action is wrong, it is wrong because it conflicts with God's nature of goodness. At the end of our conversation she did not ask me to lead her through the book of Romans. But she did thank me for sharing with her the rationality of believing in an objective moral law and, therefore, a moral lawgiver.

It is undeniable that our consciences have recognized an objective moral law. Throughout history, humans have understood that certain actions are objectively morally wrong and other behaviors are objectively morally right. Many societies understand that we should "tell the truth," "not end human life," and "do unto others as you would want them to do unto you."

Unfortunately, there have also always been moral relativists, like the Greek philosopher Protagoras, who have attempted to teach that human beings are the ones who decide the moral standard. Protagoras said, "Man (or humankind) is the measure of all things."[19]

People like Protagoras, who say there is no objective moral law (or law of human nature or rule of decent behavior), will say that if there is any moral law at all, it is subjective or relative to the individual or culture. They will say, "You have your morals, I have mine," and, "You should not impose your moral beliefs on me." Others will take the words of Christ out of context and say, "Do not judge, or you will be judged." But notice how this statement appeals to a "should not" or "do not." By their own admission, even moral relativists appeal to a transcendent standard of how one should or should not behave.

Another difficulty with this relativistic thinking is that it leaves the question, Which person is the measure of things? I would ask a moral relativist, What human being determines the standard? Is it the single mother who sacrificially provides for her three children, or is it the unfaithful, lazy guy who has left her for another woman? Is it Mother Teresa? Adolf Hitler? Gandhi? Osama bin Laden? Billy Graham?

Even though people disagree about certain aspects of the law of human nature, humankind has historically recognized the law. C. S. Lewis wrote:

> Men have differed as regards what people you ought to be unselfish to—whether it was only your own family, or your fellow countrymen, or everyone. But they have always agreed that you ought not to put yourself first. Selfishness has never been admired. Men have differed as to whether you should have one wife or four. But they have always agreed that you must not simply have any woman you liked . . . But the most remarkable thing is this. Whenever you find a man who says he does not believe in a real Right and Wrong, you will find the same man going back on this a moment later.[20]

Every law has a lawgiver. There is a moral law; therefore, it stands to reason that there is a moral lawgiver. The giver of this law is not you and it is not me. We recognize that throughout history certain societies have behaved badly, so we observe that the giver of the moral law cannot be a particular society, either. The giver of this law must be something or someone transcendent, something or someone beyond us. Dr. Martin Luther King Jr. said it this way:

> But I'm here to say to you this morning that some things are right and some things are wrong. Eternally so, absolutely so. It's wrong to hate. It always has been wrong and it always will be wrong. It's wrong in America, it's wrong in Germany, it's wrong in Russia, it's wrong in China. It was wrong in 2000 B.C., and it's wrong in 1954 A.D. It always has been wrong,

(That's right!) and it always will be wrong. (That's right!) It's wrong to throw our lives away in riotous living. No matter if everybody in Detroit is doing it, it's wrong. It always will be wrong, and it always has been wrong. It's wrong in every age, and it's wrong in every nation. Some things are right, and some things are wrong, no matter if everybody is doing the contrary. Some things in this universe are absolute. The God of the universe has made it so. And so long as we adopt this relative attitude toward right and wrong, we're revolting against the very laws of God himself.[21]

Martin Luther King Jr. strongly believed that an absolute moral law exists, and, therefore, that a moral lawgiver must exist. He called this moral lawgiver God.

The "moral argument" sums up the third reason that I trust that God is real. Although these reasons do not demand necessarily that this Being is the triune God of Christianity, it does leave suggest that some such Being exists in reality.

I'd like to add something before I end this chapter. Although this goes beyond purely intellectual reasons for God's existence, I do not feel that I could just leave you on that note of simple reasons or clues to trust God's existence. We have to be honest with ourselves as we wrestle with this issue of the moral law or the law of nature. Let's examine our own hearts and see how well we have done with keeping it.

Perhaps you feel confident that you have kept the moral law better than this person or that person, but the more we think about this, we must admit that we have not kept it consistently. Even though in one aspect we are good, being created in the image of God, morally we are very bad. Even if we have just broken part of this law of nature, just one simple law, we are still guilty. We still offend the Moral Lawgiver. And we have broken more laws than we want to admit. I am not just writing about the terrorist and the rapist. I am talking about myself. Have you, like me, been jealous, lustful, hateful, and prideful at times? There have been times that I have known the right thing to do, but I have not always done it. I have broken the moral law.

The apostle Paul shared this same struggle when he wrote a letter to the church in Rome. "For we know that the law is spiritual," he wrote, "but I am made out of flesh, sold into sin's power. For I do not understand what I am doing, because I do not practice what I want to do, but I do what I hate."[22] Have you ever been in a place like that before? You knew something was wrong, but you did it anyway. You knew you shouldn't have lied to your parents. Maybe you intended to stop after one drink or two, but you gave in again. Or, although you knew you shouldn't look at a pornographic website, you enjoyed that moment of lust. Haven't we all broken at least some of these laws and ended up doing the very thing we hate? Paul goes on to describe his struggle with trying to keep the moral law:

> So I discover this principle: when I want to do good, evil is with me. For in my inner self I joyfully agree with God's law. But I see a different law in the parts of my body, waging war against the law of my mind and taking me prisoner to the law of sin in the parts of my body. What a wretched man I am![23]

Have you ever felt wretched, defeated, and helpless? Many "positive thinking" speakers on TV will try to motivate you by saying that you are not sinful. They will say things like, "You have the truth within you," and, "You just need to change your attitude and feel good about yourself." It seems that they're just trying to put a Band-Aid on the mortal wound of spiritual seekers without sharing the real cure.

If we have been unfaithful to God and His laws, just having a positive attitude is not enough; we must humbly face the fact that we have been selfish—we have lived for ourselves rather than for God. The solution to this spiritual problem cannot come from within us. It must come from somewhere else. Paul concludes his passage about struggling against his sinful nature by giving us the solution to our problem and by pointing us in the right direction. He wrote, "Oh, what a miserable person I am! Who will free me from this life that is dominated by sin and death? Thank God! The answer is in Jesus Christ our Lord."[24]

You and I do not have to stay defeated. Even though God hates sin, he compassionately loves you. The good news is that the Moral Lawgiver took on flesh through the person of Jesus Christ to rescue you and me. You and I can trust Jesus because God has revealed himself not only as the Intelligent Designer, First Cause, and Moral Lawgiver, but He has also personally identified with sinful humans —by paying the price to rescue us, forgive us, and restore us to His favor. In later chapters we will discover that the Moral Lawgiver pursues a relationship with us and can be discovered in Jesus Christ. We may still mess up, but the Moral Lawgiver will continue to love us and help us, through His love and power, to become more like Him.

Chapter Three

· ·

Why Should I Trust Jesus When I Have Been Let Down So Many Times?

"My God, my God why have you forsaken me?
Why are you so far from saving me, so far
from the words of my groaning?"

—Psalm 22:1

As a lanky six-foot-four sophomore in high school who could barely dunk a basketball, I was desperate for help. The advertisement had led this gullible aspiring athlete to believe that my vertical jump would increase eight to twelve inches if I simply purchased and used the Strength Shoe. The Strength Shoe looked ridiculous, with an unusual bottom support piece, yet according to the ad, my athletic quickness and jumping ability were promised to increase exponentially. The shoe was designed to put strenuous tension on an athlete's calf muscle while the athlete performed exhausting exercises. So, tired of having my shots swatted by much shorter players and getting hung by the front of the rim, I took a risk, purchased the Strength Shoe, and went to work.

Neighbors were not sure about my sanity as they observed an awkward teenager wearing these ridiculous shoes, jumping and power skipping down the street. It's possible that my leaping ability increased by an inch or two, but the brutal reality was that I was destined to be an ordinary jumper.

I had a teammate at Oak Hill Academy nicknamed "Helicopter." He was seven inches shorter than I was, but he could jump at least twenty inches higher! In warm-ups, our crowds would stand up and cheer loudly whenever Helicopter would perform impressive acrobatic dunks, which can now be seen on ESPN and *And 1 Mixtape*. Usually I was next in line, and even though I always gave it my best shot, the crowds would simply get quiet and sit down during my unimpressive routine.

For several years, I placed my trust in the Strength Shoe. Those shoes were very expensive and had promised much, but in the end, they let me down. They never did what the ad had promised. My jumping ability never really improved much.

Unfortunately, sometimes Christ-followers expect God to be a magic genie-in-a-bottle God. Like me with the Strength Shoe, they think that as soon as they get on board—poof!—all of their dreams and expectations will suddenly come true.

You may have had the same experience. You were waiting for God to do something significant in your life. You were faithful in prayer. You waited in expectation, but the answer you wanted never came. Maybe you claimed a promise in the Word of God that didn't come true. Eventually, you may have even felt disappointed with God.

Although my personal illustration with the Strength Shoe was on a light note, many people have real inward struggles with broken promises. They truly trusted that God was going to do something in their life, but then it never happened. In moments of pain and uncertainty, some of these people are genuinely wondering, *Why should I trust Jesus when I have been let down so many times?*

Here are some examples:

- A single woman thought that God would bring a solid Christian man (not necessarily "Prince Charming") into her life, but years pass, and she is still single and lonely.
- A man with a troubled marriage was confident that God

was going to heal his marriage, but his wife just handed him divorce papers.

- A capable businessman thought God had given him a great business idea, but after he had invested much hard work, prayer, and capital, it failed miserably.
- A Christian family felt that through faith and prayer, God was going to heal their mother of cancer, but after lengthy treatment, she died.
- A young missionary felt that because he had sold all he had and moved his family to serve God in India, God would certainly meet his needs and open the right doors to provide for him. After six months, however, no doors opened, and all his money was gone. He returned home dejected and low on faith.

Whenever we feel that God has let us down, it can shake our trust in him. J. B. Phillips wrote:

To some people the mental image of God is a kind of blur of disappointment. "Here," they say resentfully and usually with more than a trace of self-pity, "is One whom I trusted, but He let me down." The rest of their lives is consequently shadowed by this letdown. Thenceforth there can be no mention of God, Church, religion or even parson, without starting the whole process of association of God is a Disappointment.[1]

When we have tough times, we can be sure that God is not against us,[2] nor has He forsaken us.[3] We will probably look back at the times in our lives in which unexpected or disappointing events occurred and realize that God allowed things providentially to happen that way. Sometimes we suffer because of our own foolishness or stubbornness. On other occasions, we might have been protected mysteriously from something far worse. Maybe God was redirecting our steps. Someone once said, "God directs our steps, and also our stops." As Christ-followers, Jesus calls us to trust Him when we feel His presence and things are going well. We are also called to trust Him when things do not work out exactly the way we had planned.

When Jesus called the apostle Paul to follow Him, Paul was a wealthy and influential Pharisee and a Roman citizen. Several years later, Paul had been severely beaten, whipped, stoned, and put in prison for his faith. Paul could have thought that because he had diligently preached the Word after his conversion, God would have delivered him from all of those horrible situations, but that never happened. Despite his faithful service, his fervent prayers, and his consistent love for Christ and others in the faith, Paul eventually was put to death for his trust in Jesus.

While Paul was imprisoned in Rome, he wrote a letter to a group of Christians. He said:

> I know how to live on almost nothing or with everything. I have learned the secret of living in every situation, whether it is with a full stomach or empty, with plenty or little. For I can do everything through Christ, who gives me strength.[4]

What about you and me? Are we content in every situation? Do we choose to trust Jesus even when life is not working out the way we thought it would? Can we trust Jesus even when we feel like God isn't making sense to us?

Scripture describes how, at one point, a huge crowd was following Jesus because they saw the signs and miracles that He was performing. The people had followed Him a long way and had not eaten for many hours. Out of His love for the people, Jesus performed an extraordinary miracle and fed all five thousand of them with just five barley loaves and two fish.

> When the people saw the sign He had done, they said, "This really is the Prophet who was to come into the

world!" Therefore, when Jesus knew that they were about to come and take Him by force to make Him king, He withdrew again to the mountain by Himself.[5]

The next day, the crowds found Jesus on the other side of the sea. A conversation broke out among a couple of His disciples that might have sounded like this:

> "James!"
> "What do you want, John?" replied James.
> "Brother, the crowds are ready to make Jesus king! This means that you and I will be reigning as governors! We will be rich! We will be reigning with the King!"
> "I told you, John, it was only a matter of time."

I'm only speculating about the conversations between the disciples, but we do know that Jesus was gaining popularity so rapidly that the people were ready to make Him king by force. They were fascinated with Jesus and enamored with Him. The disciples, as His close associates, probably speculated that their time of fame, popularity, and good fortune had arrived.

Jesus had the ability to communicate messages that ticked off the rich religious leaders while resonating with the ordinary folks. The common people loved His teaching. No doubt thoughts of the previous stories Jesus had told flashed back in the minds of the disciples. Perhaps He was going to tell the story of the heroic father who runs out to greet his rebellious son who had come back home. Or maybe Jesus would utter words of comfort and reassurance. But just then Jesus stood up and began to preach another message. Members of Jesus' "fan club" were not expecting the words that came out of Jesus' mouth. His words seemed offensive, even crude:

> Truly, truly, I say to you, unless you eat the flesh of the Son of Man and drink his blood, you have no life in you. Whoever

feeds on my flesh and drinks my blood has eternal life, and I will raise him up on the last day. For my flesh is true food, and my blood is true drink.[6]

What was Jesus talking about? Gross! Some people wondered if he was a cannibal. As a Christian two thousand years later, I can recognize the symbolism of this passage. It points to Christ's atoning death for us on the cross. But let's try to put ourselves in the disciples' shoes. At that point in the story, the disciples had no idea what Jesus was talking about. They didn't even understand what Jesus was talking about when He spoke of His death and resurrection.

Therefore, when many of His disciples heard this, they said, "This teaching is hard! Who can accept it?" Jesus, knowing in Himself that His disciples were complaining about this, asked them, "Does this offend you?"
From that moment many of His disciples turned back and no longer accompanied Him.[7]

Jesus had many followers who felt that they had been let down. They were thinking, *He was such a compassionate teacher and miracle worker. Why did he have to get so weird on us?* So they stopped following Jesus.

At certain times in our lives, we may feel disappointment toward God. But we must be careful not to take offense at what God does or does not do. After hours of prayer about the business deal, are we offended when it does not work out? When we pray fervently for healing, are we offended when God does not answer? Are you offended when your girlfriend or boyfriend dumps you?

We live in a culture in which most people, though they may not be Christians, consider themselves to be "spiritual." Within the new spirituality, the hip thing to do is to be disrespectful toward God when things don't make sense to us. "I'm just being real with God," we explain. "If I'm angry, I'll shake my fist or even curse God."

At one point in Elizabeth Gilbert's *New York Times* best-selling book *Eat, Pray, Love*, she curses God, and directs a rather ironic, profanity-laced tirade at the deity whose existence she has just categorically denied. Many in our culture will applaud this attitude and say, "She's so authentic."

Even when we have authentic questions about God and His work, we must be humble in our questioning. Being "real" should never be an excuse to curse God. In his psalms, King David expressed authentic emotions about his relationship with God. Yet, even in his darkest moments, he never cursed God, nor did he scream at Him with profane prayers.

In the uncertainty of our lives, when we feel frustrated or "ticked off" at God, Jesus also asks us, "Do you take offense at Me?" Our culture often tries to make God small by making Him out to be a "god" who is just a friend or a pal on par with us humans. Even though Jesus is a friend to those who trust Him, He is still the Holy God and so much greater than us. Shaking our fist at God makes as much sense as an ant shaking his fist at Shaq or Yao Ming.

I often read passages in the Bible and wonder, *What in the world does this mean?* Sometimes I ask, "God, why does it have to be this way?" But just because I don't have all the answers doesn't mean that there are no answers.

Even in moments of confusion and disappointment, Jesus Christ is still trustworthy. You may pray, "Jesus, this doesn't make sense to me right now." But remember that He backed up His offensive claims by coming back from the grave. We may not understand and know what He will do, but we do know what He has already done. He has revealed enough of His character to prove that He is worthy of our trust, regardless of the mystery.

In John's gospel, after many of the disciples deserted Jesus, He looked at the twelve and said:

"You don't want to go away too, do you?"
Simon Peter answered, "Lord, who will we go to? You

have the words of eternal life. We have come to believe and know that You are the Holy One of God!"[9]

When circumstances in life make being a Christian difficult, our response should be the same as Simon Peter's: "Lord, who will we go to?" Jesus still offers each of us the "words of eternal life." Whenever God does not make sense, we must remember that we already know enough about God to trust Him. Jesus is the Holy One who can be trusted for eternity.

I do not know exactly what will happen in your future, but I know that God has providentially done things throughout history that words cannot adequately explain. Regardless of what is happening right now in your life, following Jesus is better than anything that this world can offer. Jesus may not have revealed what He will do tomorrow, but you can get to know Him right now. We can trust Him, even in the midst of mystery and unanswered questions.

Jesus said that born of women, there was nobody greater than John the Baptist. He was a prophet. He baptized Jesus, witnessed the Holy Spirit descend on Christ like a dove, and heard the audible voice of God. Have you heard the audible voice of God? I sure haven't. Has Christ asked you to baptize Him? Me neither.

John was a first cousin of Jesus, who leaped in the womb of his mother, Elizabeth, when she saw Mary, who was pregnant with Jesus. John spent some of his earlier years knowing Jesus as his cousin. When John started his ministry, he proclaimed, "Get ready, Jesus is coming! Prepare the way for the King of all kings."

Yet, near the end of his ministry, even John the Baptist experienced feelings of disappointment with Jesus. After all, he had devoted himself to being the master of ceremonies for Jesus. What did that get him? Prison and, eventually, beheading.

Jesus didn't visit John in prison, either. So, with honest doubts about His identity, John sent word to Jesus:

"Are You the One who is to come, or should we expect someone else?"[10]

Truth be told, John was confused and maybe even offended. "Why has Jesus not dealt with the Roman authorities yet? Why hasn't Jesus done anything to get me out of prison? He could have at least paid me a visit!" Jesus, however, simply sent the word back: "Go and report to John what you hear and see: the blind see, the lame walk, those with skin diseases are healed, the deaf hear, the dead are raised, and the poor are told the good news."[11]

Jesus simply reminded John of the evidence that He had already revealed. In essence, Jesus was saying, "John, you may not understand why you are suffering and even facing a death sentence, but remember the prophecies that I have fulfilled and the miracles that I have done. You may not understand why this happening, John, but you know who I am. You know your calling. Remember, I am the Messiah, the one sent by God, and the one whom the prophets and priests have been anticipating. Do you trust Me, John?"

Later Jesus said, "Blessed is he who doesn't take offense at me." John was a man of devout faith, boldness, and prayer, and even he experienced periods of doubt and disappointment. The important thing is that John never let his doubt and disappointment turn into offense. This is a relevant reminder for you and me.

HOW SHOULD WE RESPOND TO DISAPPOINTMENT, SUFFERING, AND UNANSWERED QUESTIONS?

Focus on the goodness of God.

In moments of disappointment, we can still focus on the goodness of God. King David, who suffered much rejection as a young man, kept his focus on the goodness of God. He wrote, "I would have despaired unless I had believed that I would see the goodness of the Lord in the land of the living."[12] Paul told the church in Rome that God has the power to use even the bad things in our life to bring about good in some way. "And we know that in all things," he wrote, "God works for the good of those who love him, who have been called according to his purpose."[13]

God is still working, even when we may not see the results. The biblical figure Job was a man of integrity and purity, and yet God allowed everything to be taken from him. Job still remained faithful to God. God is good all the time. His nature is to be loving and perfect, even though we may experience terrible circumstances in life. Few of us, if any, have ever suffered as much as Job, who lost his valued possessions, all of his children, and eventually his health. Then his best friends blamed this innocent, God-fearing man for all his misfortune! Maybe we've experienced some tough times as well and received little sympathy from friends or apparent help from God. Regardless, let's focus on following the example of Job by clinging to the goodness of God. Even in the worst of times, we can continue to bless the name of the Lord.

Realize that the best is yet to come.

Many people do not trust Jesus, because the problem of evil makes them doubt the existence of God. At one level this is an emotional objection. But it is also a genuine intellectual objection that dates back to the ancient Greek philosopher Epicurus.

Using principles adapted from Epicurus and later David Hume, some atheists will state the problem of evil this way:

1. If God is all good, he would destroy evil.
2. If God is all powerful, he could destroy evil.
3. But evil is not destroyed.
4. Therefore, there is no such God.[14]

Dr. Norman Geisler gives a Christian response to this argument. Christianity holds that even though God could not destroy (annihilate) all evil without destroying all good, nevertheless, He can and will defeat (overcome) all evil without destroying free choice. The argument can be summarized as follows:

1. God is all good and desires to defeat evil.
2. God is all powerful and is able to defeat evil.
3. Evil is not *yet* defeated.
4. Therefore, it will one day be defeated.

Geisler points out that:

The infinite power and perfection of God guarantee the eventual defeat of evil. The fact that it is not yet accomplished in no way diminishes the certainty that it will be defeated. Even though evil cannot be destroyed without destroying free choice, nonetheless, it can be *overcome*.

The atheist philosopher will often hold that the two statements, "An all-powerful and all-good God exists," and, "Evil exists" are logically inconsistent. Philosopher William Lane Craig notes that there is not an *explicit* contradiction in these statements. The atheist is often assuming that if God is all good, then He would prefer to create a world without evil than to create a world in which evil exists. Dr. Craig notes that this assumption is not necessarily true:

The fact is that in many cases we allow pain and suffering to occur a person's life in order to bring about some greater good or because we have some sufficient reason for allowing it. Every parent knows this fact. There comes a point at which a parent can no longer protect his child from every scrape, bruise, or mishap; there are other times when discipline must be inflicted on the child in order to teach him to become a mature, responsible adult. Similarly, God may permit suffering in our lives to build us or to test us, or to build and test others, or to achieve some other overriding end.[15]

Currently, Jesus might be allowing you to suffer right now. He is allowing you to grow through the struggle in this fallen world. Jesus said, "In this world, you will have trouble. But take heart! I have overcome the world."[16] Paul the apostle understood this hope as he encouraged us with these words:

> For our present troubles are small and won't last very long. Yet they produce for us a glory that vastly outweighs them and will last forever! So we don't look at the troubles we can see now; rather, we fix our gaze on things that cannot be seen. For the things we see now will soon be gone, but the things we cannot see will last forever.[17]

> I consider that the sufferings of this present time are not worthy to be compared with the glory which shall be revealed in us.[18]

The grandest promises in all of Scripture are those concerning the future home for those who trust in Jesus. If we can endure our present suffering and continue to trust in the goodness of God, we have a lot to look forward to. The best is yet to come! We read in the book of Revelation:

> Then I saw a new heaven and a new earth, for the old heaven and the old earth had disappeared. And the sea was also gone. And I saw the holy city, the new Jerusalem, coming down from God out of heaven like a bride beautifully dressed for her husband. I heard a loud shout from the throne, saying, "Look, God's home is now among his people! He will live with them, and they will be his people. God himself will be with them. He will wipe every tear from their eyes, and there will be no more death or sorrow or crying or pain. All these things are gone forever."[19]

Continue to joyfully obey God.

In 586 BC, King Nebuchadnezzar of Babylon declared war on Jerusalem and besieged the city. The king ordered his chief of staff to bring to the palace some of the captive young men of Judah's royal family. "Select only strong, healthy, and good-looking young men," he said. "Make sure they are well versed in every branch of learning, are gifted with knowledge and good judgment, and are suited to serve in the royal palace. Train these young men in the language and literature of Babylon." The king assigned them a daily ration of food and wine from his own kitchens. They were to be trained for three years, and then they would enter the royal service.[20] Along with Daniel, you probably remember that Shadrach, Meshach, and Abednego were three of the young men chosen.

Then an incident occurred that would severely test the faith of these young Hebrew men.

> King Nebuchadnezzar made a gold statue ninety feet tall and sent messages to the high officers and officials and all the provincial officials to come to the dedication of the statue. When these officials came and stood before the statue King Nebuchadnezzar had set up, a herald shouted out, "People of all races and nations and languages, listen to the king's command! When you hear the sound of the horn and other musical instruments, bow to the ground to worship King Nebuchadnezzar's gold statue. Anyone who refuses to obey will immediately be thrown into a blazing furnace."[21]

Shadrach, Meshach, and Abednego had a very basic decision to make—either bow to the idol or continue to obey the almighty God. Each one of them could have gotten discouraged and said, "Why have You allowed this to happen to me, God? I have loved you and I've been faithful to You all my life, but You have allowed me to be taken captive by a wicked king. Now, my entire life is threatened." But that is not what these three young Hebrews said. They were confident that God had a plan, and even if God didn't deliver them, they were determined to continue obeying Him. They refused to bow down and worship. When confronted by the King, they responded:

> O Nebuchadnezzar, we do not need to defend ourselves before you. If we are thrown into the blazing furnace, the God whom we serve is able to save us. He will rescue us from your power, Your Majesty. But even if he doesn't, we want to make it clear to you, Your Majesty, that we will never serve your gods or worship the gold statue you have set up.[22]

When we feel let down or disappointed by God, we have a decision to make. We can either take steps away from Him by failing to trust him or take steps toward Him in obedient faith.

> Consider it pure joy, my brothers, whenever you face trials of many kinds, because you know that the testing of your faith develops perseverance. Perseverance must finish its work so that you may be mature and complete, not lacking anything.[23]

God's love for you is unfailing, and you can still trust Him. David questioned God in one of his psalms:

> How long, O Lord? Will you forget me forever?
> How long will you hide your face from me?
> How long must I wrestle with my thoughts
> and every day have sorrow in my heart? [24]

But notice that David does not stop here; he continues with a confession of faith:

> But I trust in your unfailing love;
> my heart rejoices in your salvation.

I will sing to the Lord,
for he has been good to me. [25]

In C. S. Lewis's famous work *The Screwtape Letters*, a demon named Screwtape is speaking to a younger demon named Wormwood. They are devising a plan by which they can deceive a Christian who is young in the faith. Screwtape gives Wormwood this advice:

> Do not be deceived, Wormwood. Our cause is never more in danger than when a human, no longer desiring, but still intending, to do our Enemy's will, looks round upon a universe from which every trace of Him seems to have vanished, and asks why he has been forsaken and still obeys.[26]

In moments in which we feel forsaken, when we look around the universe and feel that every trace of God has vanished, let us continue to trust and cry out to Him for help. Even if we feel He is not responsive, we can still respond like the three Hebrew young men. Let it be known to all: "My God is good. My God is Almighty. He is able to help me. He can deliver me from all my troubles. But even if He doesn't, I will not be offended. I will not deny His name. I will still bow down to Him. I will still obey Him in faith. I will declare it—Jesus Christ is Lord of all! I know my future is secure in His hands! He is Immanuel, 'God with us.' Jesus was abandoned and left naked on the Roman cross to die for us, and understands our hurts. Because of Christ's love for us, we are not abandoned. As for you and me, the best is yet to come!"

Chapter Four

Why Should I Trust Jesus When Life Seems to Be Going Just Fine without Him?

*"Trust in the Lord with all your heart and lean
not on your own understanding; in all your ways
acknowledge him, and he will make your paths straight."*

—Proverbs 3:5–6

Years ago, *60 Minutes* correspondent Steve Kroft sat down for an interview with one of America's greatest athletes and celebrities at the time, the New England Patriots quarterback Tom Brady. The interview took place at Gillette Stadium in Foxboro, Massachusetts. Here is an excerpt.

KROFT: This whole experience—this whole upward trajectory—what have you learned about yourself? What kind of an effect does it have on you?

BRADY: Well, I put incredible amounts of pressure on me. When you feel like you're ultimately responsible for everyone and everything, even though you have no control over it, and you still blame yourself if things don't go right—I mean, there's a lot of pressure. A lot of times I think I get very frustrated and introverted, and there are times where I'm not the person that I want to be.

Why do I have three Super Bowl rings, and still think there's something greater out there for me? I mean, maybe a lot of people would say, "Hey man, this is what it is." I reached my goal, my dream, and my life. Me, I think, *God, it's gotta be more than this.* I mean, this can't be what it's all cracked up to be. I mean, I've done it. I'm twenty-seven. And what else is there for me?

KROFT: What's the answer?

BRADY: I wish I knew. I wish I knew.

Over fifteen hundred years ago, another man of influence experienced the same problem. Like Tom Brady, he had money and success. He was a natural leader, good looking, and a role model to young people. People respected him. Cities, churches, academic buildings, and streets bear his name today. We hear his words echoed in books, movies, and music. A popular hip-hop artist named Usher adapted his work from this man's spiritual autobiography and called his music album *Confessions.* The album reached number one on the charts.

The author of the original *Confessions* and the classic *City of God* was none other than the African-born church father and bishop Augustine. However, Augustine did not always trust Jesus, even though many looked to him as a good teacher. In fact, his original *Confessions* was perhaps more graphic, lustful, and shameful than the more recent adaptations. Ironically, fifteen hundred years later, Augustine is considered by millions to be a saint. Why?

Augustine shares in his *Confessions* his story of why he did not always trust Jesus. Augustine, a very successful professor of rhetoric in his twenties, didn't see the need to trust Jesus. In fact, Augustine was flat-out bored with the Bible. He once said, "When I turned toward the Scriptures, they appeared to be quite unworthy to be compared with the dignity of Tully (Cicero)."[1]

Augustine did not always believe in the God of the Bible. He was aware of God from the time he was a child because of the influence of his Christian mother, Monica. But he resisted her faith. Throughout his early life, Augustine achieved a great deal of success, and when exposed to Christianity, he skeptically doubted why he might need to trust in Jesus. Nevertheless, Augustine began to feel a restlessness, searching for something "greater."

Like Augustine, some people initially do not think they need to trust Jesus, because everything seems to be going well without Him. They may be somewhat knowledgeable about Christianity or spiritual matters. But then, when things still seem to be going well on the outside, they feel that something is lacking on the inside. Like Augustine, they feel restless, doubting, seeking *something*, but they don't know what it is.

Perhaps they thought that the pleasures and pursuits of this world would satisfy, but then they discovered that they really don't. In the vein of Augustine, they realized, "Our hearts are restless until they rest in you."[2] They recognized:

- Money cannot satisfy.
- Honor cannot satisfy.
- Fame cannot satisfy.
- Having a healthy body and mind cannot satisfy.
- Pleasure and the pursuit of happiness cannot satisfy.
- In summary, nothing on this earth can satisfy.

Have you ever been at a place where you thought, *If I just had that, I'd be happy*? If you just had that woman (or man), that job, that promotion, that dream house, that luxury car, or that big lottery check, it would make your life complete?

Augustine discloses his own struggle with his pursuit of those things in *Confessions*. As a brilliant young student, he excelled in the Latin classics. His parents sent him to Carthage, the prominent North African city, in 370, when he was sixteen, where he received the best education available at the time. He studied rhetoric and investigated a variety of philosophies and religions. And Carthage offered distractions, entertainment, and all the vices associated with a bustling port city.

You'll probably be surprised to know that Augustine lived with his girlfriend for ten years and had an illegitimate son by her, but he didn't love her enough to marry her. During this time, he also joined the intellectual religious cult of Manichaeism—a group that believed that reality consists of two limited gods who conflict with each other.

All through his time of rebellion, Augustine's mother cried out to the Lord to rescue Augustine from his disobedience. Can you think of a time when you were running from God, but during that period of spiritual darkness in your life, someone fervently lifted up prayers for you? Maybe your mother, father, grandmother, grandfather, pastor, teacher, neighbor, coach, or friend interceded for you. Years later, Augustine realized how important his mother's prayers had been:

> Nevertheless, O God, You stretched out Your hand from above and drew my soul out of the profound darkness of Manichaeism, because my mother, Your faithful one, wept to You on my behalf more than most mothers weep after the bodily deaths of their children. For by the light of faith and the Spirit she received from You, she saw that I was dead. You heard her, O Lord, and did not reject her tears as they poured down and watered the earth under her wherever she prayed. Yes, Lord, You truly did heed her prayers.[3]

If you're following the same path that Augustine was, most likely someone who loves you is concerned about the spiritual implications of your choices. Augustine wrote:

> My mother disapproved and warned me privately with great concern, not to have sex outside of marriage, but above all, never to defile another man's wife. My mother's appeals seemed to be but womanish counsels, which I would have blushed to obey. Yet they were from You, O God, and I knew it not. I thought that You were silent and that it was only she

who spoke. Yet it was through her that You did not keep silence toward me. Furthermore, in rejecting her counsel I was rejecting You. Yes I, her son, the son of Your handmaid, Your servant.[4]

At Monica's request, Ambrose (the Bishop of Milan) befriended Augustine. Although Augustine was impressed by the bishop's authentic Christianity, his desire to follow his passions was so strong that he could not bring himself to change his lifestyle. He wasn't willing to give up his sexual sin completely, even though he knew that it was wrong. He prayed, "Lord, help me to be pure, but not yet."[5] Then, giving up any pretense about trying to become morally pure, he took another mistress.

The more Augustine sinned, the more he realized he had no power on his own to break away from those sins. One day, in a state of turmoil, he cried out, "How long, O Lord? What will be the end to my uncleanness?" As he sobbed, he heard a group of children playing a game on the other side of the garden wall. As a part of their game, they said, "Pick up and read; pick up and read." Augustine interpreted this as a word of God being communicated to him. He returned to a spot where he had thrown down a copy of the New Testament Scriptures. He opened it and read these words from Romans: "But put ye on the Lord Jesus Christ, and make not provision for the flesh, to fulfill the lusts thereof."[6]

As he read the Scripture, he said that "a light of security flooded my soul, and all the gloom of doubt vanished away." Through that Word of God, the living Savior took control of Augustine's heart when he was thirty-two. For the first time, Augustine truly experienced the wonder of God's mercy, the beauty of Christ, and freedom from sin and shame. And, by the grace of the cross, Jesus' sacrifice broke the dominion of sin in Augustine's life.

You may not realize it, but a spiritual battle is raging for your soul at this very moment. The apostle Peter wrote, "Dear friends, I urge you, as aliens and strangers in the world, to abstain from sinful desires, which war against your soul."[7] Maybe there are sins in your life that you don't know how you can live without. Trusting Jesus involves change, because He might call you to give up a certain behavior or habit that you feel dependent upon. But no matter what you're going through, you can trust Jesus and your life will be changed for the better, just like Augustine's was. Listen to the words of the apostle Paul, the man who inspired Augustine's conversion.

> Now when a man works, his wages are not credited to him as a gift, but as an obligation. However to the man who does not work but trusts God who justifies the wicked, his faith is credited as righteousness.[8]

Augustine realized that Jesus is trustworthy and much better than anything that this world has to offer. He began his *Confessions* by worshiping the One who is trustworthy:

> To praise you is the desire of man, a little piece of your creation. You stir to take pleasure in praising you, because you have made us for yourself, and our heart is restless until it rests in you.[9]

Think about it—what would it be like to experience true inner peace and rest? No more working. No more striving. No more emptiness. No more restlessness. Jesus offers this to all who have become weary and disappointed in their empty pursuits. He says, "Come to me, all you who are weary and burdened, and I will give you rest. Take my yoke upon you and learn from me, for I am gentle and humble in heart, and you will find rest for your souls."[10]

THE MAN WHO HAD IT ALL

Long before Augustine, another man learned that the best this world can offer gives no lasting contentment or inner happiness. If ever a man had it all, King Solomon fit the bill.

Solomon, ruler over Israel around three thousand years ago, was one of the wealthiest and wisest people who ever lived. He authored over three thousand proverbs (wise sayings), a thousand songs, and many scientific works on botany and zoology. As a master architect, Solomon oversaw the construction of one of the grandest buildings of all time—the temple in Jerusalem. People from all over the earth came to hear his great wisdom, which they described "as measureless as the sand on the seashore."[11] They also marveled over his great wealth and his spectacular building projects.

When Solomon began his reign over Israel, he had a humble heart. He sought a greater measure of God's wisdom, and the Lord blessed him with wisdom beyond measure. But as Solomon grew older, he allowed his heart to turn away from the living God to the false gods of his many wives from foreign lands. Near the end of his life, after achieving great political success and gaining everything the world had to offer, Solomon wrote Ecclesiastes, which revealed his frustration and utter dissatisfaction with all the "good things" in life.

Sounds familiar, doesn't it? Ecclesiastes probes the meaning of life, only to expose our inability to find meaning and significance in life apart from God. Eugene Peterson, a gifted author, biblical linguist, and translator, commented about the book of Ecclesiastes:

> It is our propensity to go off on our own, trying to be human by our own devices and desires, that makes Ecclesiastes necessary reading. Ecclesiastes sweeps our souls clean of all "lifestyle" spiritualities so that we can be ready for God's visitation revealed in Jesus Christ. . . . It is an exposé and rejection of every arrogant and ignorant expectation that we can live our lives by ourselves on our own terms.[12]

Solomon wrote of all his worldly pursuits and pleasures:

I said to myself, "Let's go for it—experiment with pleasure, have a good time!" But there was nothing to it, nothing but smoke.
What do I think of the fun-filled life? Insane! Inane! My verdict on the pursuit of happiness? Who needs it?
With the help of a bottle of wine and all the wisdom I could muster, I tried my level best to penetrate the absurdity of life. I wanted to get a handle on anything useful we mortals might do during the years we spend on this earth.
Oh, I did great things: built houses, planted vineyards, designed gardens and parks and planted a variety of fruit trees in them, made pools of water to irrigate the groves of trees.
I bought slaves, male and female, who had children, giving me even more slaves; then I acquired large herds and flocks, larger than any before me in Jerusalem. I piled up silver and gold, loot from kings and kingdoms. I gathered a chorus of singers to entertain me with song and—the most exquisite of all pleasures—voluptuous maidens for my bed.
Oh, how I prospered! I left all my predecessors in Jerusalem far behind, left them behind in the dust. What's more, I kept a clear head through it all. Everything I wanted I took—I never said no to myself. I gave in to every impulse, held back nothing. I sucked the marrow of pleasure out of every task—my reward to myself for a hard day's work![13]

Let's bring this example into the present. Say that a thirty-year-old entrepreneur is riding a limousine in New York City with an entourage of bodyguards. This young CEO, Ivy League graduate, and upcoming politician has recently inherited a multibillion-dollar fortune from a family member whom he barely knew. Now he's the richest person in the world. He is dating a variety of gorgeous supermodels, owns the most extravagant homes, and hires the best entertainers to perform private concerts at his mansions.

Most people in our society would think, *Sounds great, doesn't it?* But do you think this young character would really be happy? King Solomon enjoyed a similar lifestyle, yet he felt frustrated and dissatisfied. Solomon concluded this section with despair:

> Then I took a good look at everything I'd done, looked at all the sweat and hard work. But when I looked, I saw nothing but smoke. Smoke and spitting into the wind. There was nothing to any of it. Nothing.[14]

Clearly, Solomon's deepest inner needs were not being met by all the world's pleasures. His emotions were starved for true love, not just sensual pleasure. His heart longed for true fulfillment, not just selfish indulgence in material things. And, most of all, His spirit was starved for a right relationship with the Lord.

Lessons from Augustine, Solomon, and Others Who Trust God

We may feel that all is fine, and yet be deceived by the uncertainty of wealth.[15]

"There is a way that seems right to a man, but in the end it leads to death," wrote Solomon.[16] Feelings come and feelings go. Sometimes feelings can be deceiving. A person may feel just fine living life without trusting Christ, and yet be deceived by the temporal whirlwind of wealth and pleasure.

Certainly God wants us to have pleasure and enjoy creation. After all, creation is one of God's gifts to us. There's nothing wrong with us enjoying the beautiful, positive aspects of life. In addition, there's nothing wrong with working, earning money, and spending that money on the things that we need. Scripture does not say that money is the root of all evil; it says that "the *love* of money is a root of all kinds of evil."[17] Money itself is morally neutral; it's not bad or evil in and of itself. However, the Scriptures instruct young leaders "not to put their hope in wealth, which is so uncertain, but to put their hope in God, who richly provides us with everything for our enjoyment."[18]

As a high school teacher at a private school and a part-time grad student, I've sometimes felt poor working in Plano, Texas. If you visit the private school where I teach, you can tell right away which parking lot holds the teachers' and staff's cars, and which one holds the students' vehicles. If you see a lot full of shiny new BMWs, Cadillac Escalades, and Hummers, you know you aren't looking at the teachers' parking section.

I sometimes have a selfish desire to have more. I'd love to have more resources so I wouldn't have to struggle with certain things. Yet when I begin to feel discontent, God convicts me and reminds me that one billion people on this planet live on less than a dollar a day. Hundreds of millions of people don't even have access to clean drinking water. Most of the world would look at me and think I am wealthy.[19]

We should never take pride or boast in what we can accomplish. But when God blesses us (which He has), we need to bless others in the same way. Scripture says, "You may say to yourself, 'My power and the strength of my hands have produced this wealth for me.' But remember the Lord your God, for it is He who gives you the ability to produce wealth."[20] I used to think that verse was written only for the rich people in America, but now I know that this verse is talking about me, too.

Having more things does not ensure more happiness.

I've been invited by friends on many occasions to participate in mission trips. God always reminds me on these trips how much He loves the world.

Several years ago, I spent my spring break in Cote d'Ivoire, Africa. One of the reasons for my journey across the Atlantic Ocean was to join a group of friends who were donating a purification system for drinking water. One day, I journeyed into the city to hand out small bottles of bubble soap to the children to play with. These young boys and girls had a lot going against them, but I wish you could have seen the expressions of happiness on their faces.

Some of these children suffered from guinea worm disease or other illnesses because of contamination in the water. Although many were hurting physically, they radiated joy, peace, and inexpressible satisfaction. They seemed so much happier than their American counterparts. Happy smiles lit the faces of these little children—simply over a tiny bottle of bubbles.

However, I believe that their satisfaction wasn't really about bubbles. Joy overflowed in these kids' hearts long before they received the bubbles. I believe the pleasure in their souls was because of their simple and genuine trust in God.

Education, health, and wealth are important for the good of society, but we don't find real satisfaction in these things. Like Augustine and King Solomon before him, one of the great thinkers of the 17th century, Blaise Pascal, said, "There is a God-shaped vacuum in the heart of every man, which cannot be filled by any created thing, but only by God, the Creator, made known through Jesus." True happiness comes in knowing, trusting, and experiencing God. Nothing else can fill us up.

We must not resist inner restlessness or conviction of the soul.

Imagine a young deer running from a blazing forest fire. The fire has been on his heels for hours; his heart is racing and his insides feel like they're going to explode. Finally he reaches a wide, cool running stream that stops the fire. Finally he can rest and drink deeply of the refreshing water. What a delight! What satisfaction after such an awful experience. This is the setting for this particular psalm:

> As the deer pants for streams of water, so my soul pants for you, O God.
> My soul thirsts for God, for the living God.[21]

Finding God can be just as refreshing for our souls as a cool stream of water is for a desperate deer. If we sense an inner restlessness, it may be God's Spirit prompting us to respond to Him. The prophet Isaiah wrote, "Seek the Lord while He may be found; call on him while he is near."[22] God will draw us and will provide the way, but He also has given us free will to respond to Him. It's up to us to earnestly seek Him.

We can give thanks to God for temporal pleasures but fix our thoughts ultimately on eternal pleasures found in Christ.

"So we fix our eyes not on what is seen, but on what is unseen. For what is seen is temporary, but what is unseen is eternal."[23] Scripture tells us that if we only live for the pleasures and pursuits of this present life, we will be sure to have some fun along the way; but we will miss out on a much greater pleasure. Jesus asked, "What good is it for a man to gain the whole world, yet forfeit his soul?"[24] Some people seem to consider God some kind of "cosmic killjoy" who never wants us to have a good time. Nothing could be further from the truth. God created us to have pleasure on this earth. But God doesn't want us to settle for secondary pleasures that take us away from the greatest pleasure discovered in Him. Jesus said, "I have come that they may have life, and they may have it more abundantly."[25] Solomon said, "There is nothing better for a man, than that he should eat and drink, and that his soul should enjoy good in his labor. This also, I saw, was from the hand of God."[26] So enjoy your work, but remember that your greatest satisfaction should be found in loving God and loving people. Scripture says, "You have made known to me the path of life; you will fill me with joy in your presence, with eternal pleasures at your right hand.[27]

Another young leader in the Bible, Moses, became the right-hand man of Pharaoh, who was the ruler of Egypt, the greatest nation on earth at that time. Moses had at his disposal all the wealth and pleasures that a man could want. Yet God called him to a greater destiny and purpose. God called Moses to perform a duty of eternal consequence, and Moses made the difficult choice to obey the Lord. Scripture says:

> It was by faith that Moses, when he grew up, refused to be called the son of Pharaoh's daughter. He chose to share the oppression of God's people instead of enjoying the fleeting pleasures of sin. He thought it was better to suffer for the sake of Christ than to own the treasures of Egypt, for he was looking ahead to his great reward.[28]

How about you and me? Sometimes we need to be willing to make the difficult choice to say no to some of the temporary pleasures this world bombards us with and say yes to greater eternal pleasures that found in Jesus Christ. Unfortunately we sometimes settle for sub-par pleasures, as C. S. Lewis observed:

> If we consider the unblushing promises of reward and the staggering nature of the rewards promised in the Gospels, it would seem that our Lord finds our desires not too strong, but too weak. We are half-hearted creatures, fooling about with drink and sex and ambition when infinite joy is offered us, like an ignorant child who wants to go on making mud pies in a slum because he cannot imagine what is meant by the offer of a holiday at the sea. We are far too easily pleased.[29]

Consider just a few of the promises God offers us for both now and in the life to come:

- Inexpressible and glorious joy[30]
- Abundant life[31]
- Peace that surpasses understanding[32]
- True riches[33]
- Eternal pleasures[34]

Wow! Who would want to exchange such incredible promises for the "mud pies" of temporary pleasure? True happiness in this life comes in knowing, trusting, and experiencing Christ. Nothing else can fill us up. Those who say yes to Him will store up future treasure and even now begin to "experience real life."[35] Don't settle for less than God's best!

Chapter Five

. . . .

Why Should I Trust Jesus When All I Need to Do Is Trust Myself?

"He who trusts in himself is a fool."

—Proverbs 28:26

Have you ever read a book that looked at first glance like a good Christian book, but as you read more, you started questioning whether the message was really true? As I was browsing the New Age and Spiritual section at Barnes & Noble, I saw *A Course in Miracles* by the deceased Helen Schucman, bestselling books endorsed by Oprah Winfrey, and other self-help titles by authors like Marianne Williamson and Wayne Dyer. Then I saw a book by Deepak Chopra, endorsed by Dr. Harvey Cox, a professor of divinity at Harvard. Cox wrote:

> *The Third Jesus* has now long since escaped the confines of church, Christianity, and even "religions." Chopra's book thoughtfully presents a Jesus who is paradoxically both closer to the original and more available to post-modern people than the stained glass version.[1]

Because this book talked about Jesus, I was curious to look it over. Inside I discovered ideas like the following: "The experience of God turns into a constant for one reason alone: 'I' and 'God' become one and the same, and "If I sense the presence of God, then in some way I have entered God's identity and taken it as my own. Were it not for this quality of union, Jesus' message would not be realized."

Chopra implies that by learning to trust yourself, you are "taking on God's identity," and that this is the same as trusting Jesus. You, Jesus, God, and the universe are one and the same. Some call this "Christ-consciousness." Immediately, I realized that this book was not teaching the gospel message taught by the Jesus I trusted. Instead, it promoted pantheism.

The word *pantheism* literally means "all (*pan*) is God (*theism*)."[2] Pantheism is a widespread spiritual belief. Two billion people on planet Earth—approximately one out of every three people in the world—is a pantheist. So it's crucial for us to understand the dangers of this worldview and to realize why we need to trust the real Jesus.

Although there are differences among pantheistic views, most pantheists believe that God and the universe are one and the same. Pantheism teaches that you must overcome the illusions of sense experience and trust the truth within yourself.

Many pantheists may not be aware of the history of their beliefs; in fact, they may be unfamiliar with the term *pantheism*. Ted Cabal, a professor of philosophy at Southern Seminary, commented about some American pantheists, "They prefer the practice of spirituality over organized religion. They believe that no single religious teacher can claim the allegiance of all; claims by Jesus as being *the* Way must be reinterpreted or rejected altogether."[3] Cabal continued, "Mixing and matching the objects of worship, [pantheists] often identify themselves simultaneously in terms such as Buddhist, Jewish, and Presbyterian." Pantheism teaches that "everything is One," and "the One is God." It teaches that "I am God. You are God. The universe is God. We are all God." Dr. Norman Geisler explains pantheism in this way:

> The primary teaching of absolute pantheism is that humans must overcome their ignorance and realize that they are God. Those who put a distance between God and humanity teach a dualistic view of the person—a body and soul. The body

holds the human down, keeping him or her from uniting with God. So each must purge his or her body so the souls can be released to attain oneness with the Absolute One. For all pantheists, the chief goal or end of humanity is to unite with God.[4]

The largest religion with a pantheistic worldview is Hinduism. From Zen Buddhism to the philosophy of G.W.F. Hegel, from many yoga classes at health clubs to the ideas of Oprah Winfrey, from movies like *Star Wars* to New Age poetry and thousands of spiritual "self-help" and "inspirational" books, the pantheistic movement has always had its advocates. But the worldview has recently been spreading rapidly in the United States. In fact, many Christian leaders are beginning to incorporate pantheistic thought into their teaching without even recognizing it. We hear echoes of pantheistic thought in Christian churches when the lyrics of worship songs say things like, "God is the ground," "God is the air I breathe," and "God is the universe." When I was in seminary, Dr. Geisler expressed his concern about pantheistic ideas creeping into churches. He encouraged worship leaders to be careful that their songs have words of truth. He said, "If you don't know the difference between, 'God made the ground' and 'God is the ground,' you shouldn't be leading worship in church!"

Marianne Williamson has written a commentary on Helen Schucman's work, *A Course in Miracles*. On the XM radio channel *Oprah and Friends*, Williamson explained the first lesson by saying, "Spiritual transformation begins with shifting your physical perceptions of what's real. If you think what you see and hear is all that's real, you'll be dictated by the limits of your senses."[5] She instructed her audience to respond, "My salvation comes from me. Nothing outside of me can hold me back. Within me is the world's salvation and my own."[6] These teachings differ greatly from that of the New Testament, which says that salvation comes not from ourselves but from God, who is a different being than us.

Pantheism is also being tolerated by some Christian authors. One Christian author expresses this tolerance in his bestselling book when he writes, "I once listened to an Indian on television say that God was in the wind and the water, and I wondered at how beautiful that was because it meant you could swim in Him or have Him brush your face in a breeze." I will leave this author unnamed because I don't think this particular author is a true pantheist. However, I do find it ironic how so many of the "younger evangelicals" who are my age are so tolerant of false doctrines like pantheism, while at the same time they are extremely intolerant of certain older conservative Christian groups that teach that the truth about reality is knowable. These younger evangelicals may appear progressively open-minded, but in reality they are just as narrow-minded as the fundamentalist, in their own way.

One of the bestselling authors of our time, Dan Brown, expresses pantheism through his character Peter Solomon in *The Lost Symbol*:

> In fact, man's oldest spiritual quest was to perceive his own entanglement, to sense his own interconnection with all things. He has always wanted to become "one" with the universe . . . to achieve the state "at-one-ment." To this day, Jews and Christians still strive for "atonement" . . . although most us have forgotten it is actually "at-one-ment" we're seeking.[7]

Another confusing aspect of pantheism is the fact that many pantheists use language about Jesus and spirituality that sounds similar to the teachings of Christianity. However, the basis of their theology contradicts the Bible's foundational truths about Christ. For example, the book *A Course in Miracles* brazenly expounds, "How mad to think that you could be condemned, and that the holy Son of God can die!"[8] This book also claims that knowledge of God is impossible: "Oneness is simply the idea God is. And in His Being, He encompasses all things. No mind holds anything but Him. We say 'God is,' and then we cease to speak, for in that knowledge words are meaningless."[9] And again, "We cannot speak nor write nor even think of this at all."

This final statement itself is self-defeating. Why does Marianne Williamson bother to speak and write at all if her words are meaningless? And why do instructors of pantheism and others teach us to think on these things? Why don't they simply obey their own instructions, say "God is," and then stop talking? If they were to follow their own advice, they could not publish book after book, write blog after blog, and continue talking about spirituality and God on their television shows. Do you think that Oprah Winfrey will ever host a spiritual discussion in which she doesn't use words? These pantheists and "New Thought" leaders may want *you* to be quiet, but they will never heed their own advice.

Pantheism contradicts what Jesus Christ taught. In pantheistic thought, Jesus and I are equal and the same; therefore, trusting Him is essentially the same as trusting myself, because we are one. However, Christianity teaches that we are distinct from God. The list below, adapted from the *Baker Encyclopedia of Christian Apologetics*, shows how Christianity differs radically from pantheism (whether it is your local yoga instructor or director George Lucas, the creator of *Star Wars*):

- Pantheism teaches that God is ultimately impersonal. In contrast, the true Jesus said that God is personal.
- The belief of pantheism attempts to violate the simple laws of logic. Christianity believes that logic is undeniable. Pantheism is self-defeating because it attempts to use logic to show that logic does not exist. Dr. Geisler notes, "When Zen Buddhist D.T. Suzuki says that to comprehend life we must abandon logic, he uses logic in his affirmation and applies it to reality."[10]
- Pantheism teaches that the universe is God; Jesus teaches that God made the universe.

- Pantheism teaches that the universe is eternal. Christianity teaches that the universe is not eternal but had a beginning in time and space.
- Pantheism says that because you are so special, you actually are a part of God. Jesus says that God created us to be special, but we have limitations and are separate from Him. We have been created in the image of God, but we are not God.
- Pantheists will avoid talking about sin. Instead, they emphasize the power of positive thinking and say that sin and evil are "illusions." The Bible says that sin and evil exist in reality. We also have inherited a sinful nature from the moment of conception. We naturally tend to be selfish creatures, walking independently of God's will.[11]
- Pantheism encourages a person to seek spirituality but not necessarily absolute truth. The real Jesus Christ wants us to love Him not only in spirit but also in truth.[12]

In order for us to know God, we must have accurate thoughts. A. W. Tozer said:

What comes into our minds when we think about God is the most important thing about us. The history of mankind will probably show that no people have risen above its religion, and man's spiritual history will positively demonstrate that no religion has ever been greater than its idea of God. Worship is pure or base as the worshiper entertains high or low thoughts of God.[13]

In our pursuit of God, we must be willing to face reality. Just because some of our friends sincerely *believe* in certain spiritual ideas, this does not mean that such spiritual ideas are necessarily true. Or, we may disbelieve something, yet be confronted with abundant evidence to the contrary. For example, pantheists believe that evil, pain, and sickness are just an "illusion." Yet if evil and sickness are not real, then where does the illusion of pain come from? What happens when someone cuts his finger badly and pain shoots through his body? Does he not shriek, cuss, or run for help? Such pantheistic philosophers attempt to play games with words, but they refuse to face reality.

We must be humble and honest enough to admit what is real and what is not. When scholar and apologist R. C. Sproul was once asked, "What is the difference between the Christian God and the gods of other religions?" Sproul noted that the main difference is this: "The God of Christianity exists."[14]

WE NEED BOTH SPIRITUALITY AND TRUTH

In the New Testament, we meet a woman who was interested in spirituality and was also searching for truth. For the majority of her life, she had trusted herself. She may have thought that she had the truth within her. She trusted her own judgment in relationships and wrongly trusted in men. But after some bad experiences, she lost trust and got divorced—five times. At this point, she began to realize that the truth was *not* within her, nor did it reside in the men that she had put her hope in for so long. She began craving something spiritual, something transcendent, something beyond her. She finally found the answer to her heart's cry in Jesus. This account is recorded in the gospel of John.

> Jesus, worn out from His journey, sat down at the well. It was about six in the evening . . . "Give Me a drink," Jesus said to her, for His disciples had gone into town to buy food.
>
> "How is it that You, a Jew, ask for a drink from me, a Samaritan woman?" she asked Him. For Jews do not associate with Samaritans.
>
> Jesus answered, "If you knew the gift of God, and who is saying to you, 'Give Me a drink,' you would ask Him, and He would give you living water."[15]

The first thing that Jesus wanted to talk to this woman about was water. Why water? Well, obviously Jesus was thirsty, but He wanted to communicate something else to her, something more profound. Water is something that everybody is dependent on. Around 70 percent of the earth's surface is covered by water, and over half of your body is made up of water. Water is so necessary that Thales, one of the first ancient Greek philosophers, believed that reality was ultimately water. Ritual washing with water is a significant part of many religions, including Hinduism, Islam, Taoism, and Judaism.

But Jesus was talking about something completely different. He was speaking of something called "living water."

> "Sir," said the woman, "You don't even have a bucket, and the well is deep. So where do You get this 'living water'? You aren't greater than our father Jacob, are You? He gave us the well and drank from it himself, as did his sons and livestock."
>
> Jesus said, "Everyone who drinks from this water will get thirsty again. But whoever drinks from the water that I will give will never get thirsty again—ever! In fact, the water I will give him will become a well of water springing up within him."[16]

The water that Jesus was speaking of represented the Holy Spirit that He would give to those who trust Him. Every person on earth has a spiritual thirst for something that will satisfy. As we mentioned in a previous chapter, Blaise Pascal called this thirst the "God-shaped vacuum." We may try to use a variety of worldly methods to fill that void, but only God's Spirit can truly satisfy. God is here with us because He is Spirit. But contrary to what pantheism teaches, God is distinct from us. The Bible teaches that God's presence is here with us in this room, but God is not the room, He is not the air, He is not the ground. We must ask the One (God) who is transcendent (greater than us) to fill us with the Holy Spirit.

Even after God fills us with His Holy Spirit, we are still distinct from Him. We have a relationship with Jesus and He certainly is our friend, but we are not the same person as He is. We do not become Jesus. Jesus says that God is still our Lord and King. Even though we are created in His image, He is a different *kind* of Being than we are. God is frequently called the Holy One, which means He is separate and distinct from mankind. He is higher and greater than anything we can relate to in our experience.

> The Lord is exalted over all the nations, his glory above the heavens.
> Who is like the Lord our God, the One who sits enthroned on high, who stoops down to look on the heavens and the earth?"[17]

> "For my thoughts are not your thoughts, neither are your ways my ways," declares the Lord. "As the heavens are higher than the earth, so are my ways higher than your ways and my thoughts than your thoughts."[18]

We can trust in God because He is so much greater than we are! Amazingly, this great and awesome God is ready to restore us to His favor and even call us His friends! We may not comprehend Him, but we can know Him and He allows our knowledge of Him to continually increase as we grow in our relationship with Him. Through Jesus, we learn to connect with God in both spirit and truth. Jesus offers this same "living water" today to any who will come to Him. He says:

> If anyone is thirsty, let him come to me and drink.[19]
> Is anyone thirsty? Come and drink even if you have no money! . . . It's all free![20]
> Whoever is thirsty, let him come; and whoever wishes, let him take the free gift of the water of life.[21]

Three Reasons to Trust Jesus instead of Ourselves

Here are three truths that will help you learn to trust Jesus instead of depending on yourself.

We are limited in knowledge, but Jesus Christ is all knowing.

Human knowledge is real, but it has its limitations. Jesus, however, is all-knowing. He knows everything about me. He knows everything about you. He knows what you are thinking. He knows what you are feeling. He understands you better than you understand yourself.

In the story about the Samaritan woman who had five husbands, Jesus, without ever meeting her before this encounter, told her the detailed truth about her past. She later testified to her neighbors, "He told me everything I ever did."[22] Jesus knew all of the embarrassing details about her, but He still loved her. Jesus knows the embarrassing details about us, but He loves us, too. Because of His mercy, He would rather redeem us than expose us.

We see evidence of Jesus' omniscience in another encounter. When a Jewish man named Nathanael saw Jesus for the first time, Jesus immediately indicated he knew him well. Nathanael asked Jesus, "How do you know me?"

"Before Philip called you, when you were under the fig tree, I saw you," Jesus answered.

"Rabbi," Nathanael replied, "You are the Son of God!" You are the King of Israel!"

Jesus responded to him, "Do you believe only because I told you I saw you under the fig tree? You will see greater things than this." Then He said, "I assure you: You will see heaven opened and the angels of God ascending and descending on the Son of Man."[23]

Even though Jesus had never personally met Nathanael, Jesus knew his name, where he was from, and even the depths of his heart. The Bible says, "The eyes of the Lord are everywhere, keeping watch on the wicked and the good."[24] God is "perfect in knowledge."[25] His understanding is "inexhaustible and boundless."[26] He even knows the number of hairs on your head.[27] That's why it's so important for us to trust in Christ, "in whom are hidden all the treasures of wisdom and knowledge."[28] Though Christ knows all about you, even the depths of your heart, He still loves you with an indescribable love.

We had nothing to with our creation; Jesus Christ designed us and sustains us.

You can also trust Jesus rather than yourself because Jesus specifically designed and created you. Scientifically speaking, you may think, "No, He didn't, my parents are responsible!" We will loosely adapt some terminology from Aristotle and say that Jesus is the *efficient cause* of your existence. Your parents were the *instrumental cause* that God used to form your existence. Ultimately, God is responsible.

Some parents may believe they "made a mistake" regarding the birth of a child. But God makes no mistakes. Even in cases of pregnancy that result from a one-night stand or rape, God still orchestrates good. The Bible says, "We know that all things work together for the good of those who love God."[29] Not everything is good, but God has the ability to produce goodness from human mistakes. The apostle Paul described Jesus as the creator and designer of everything (including you) in his letter to the church at Colossae:

> [Jesus] is the image of the invisible God,
> The firstborn over all creation,
> Because by Him everything was created,
> In heaven and on earth, the visible and the invisible,

Whether thrones or dominions or rulers or authorities—
All things have been created through Him and for Him.[30]

Jesus ultimately designed you and made no mistakes with your body or mind. The Scripture says you are "God's work of art."[31] Another translation says, "We are God's masterpiece."[32] Each of us is a unique creation, one-of-a-kind, and with God there is no shoddy workmanship, no junk. Because He lovingly created us and has ongoing plans for our lives, we can trust Him. King David wrote:

> For it was You who created my inward parts;
> You knit me together in my mother's womb.
> I will praise you because I have been remarkably and
> wonderfully made.
> Your works are wonderful, and I know this very well.[33]

Do you know this very well—that Jesus, the creator of the universe, designed you? Pantheism gives us a limited and false view of God that says He *is all*. The Bible says that Jesus *made all*. He made you, and you are special—remarkably and wonderfully made because Jesus uniquely designed you. Because of this, you can trust Him.

We are constantly changing, but Jesus Christ does not change.

Pantheism teaches that change is an illusion. This defies common sense. Even some pantheists vote for politicians who promise to bring change. Change can be good, but sometimes change can be harmful. Unfortunately, sometimes we as human beings are not perfectly consistent in loving our neighbors. In weak moments, we sometimes say unkind things or act in ways that we later regret. We might have good intentions, but we can easily be quite fickle. But God is unchanging. Scripture tells us:

> "I, the Lord, do not change."[34]
> "If we are faithless, he will remain faithful."[35]

"Jesus Christ is the same yesterday and today and forever."[36]

This biblical truth highlights one of the deep flaws of pantheist belief, as Dr. Norman Geisler explains:

> Absolute pantheism is self defeating. The absolute pantheist claims: I am God. But God is the changeless Absolute. However, humanity goes through the process of change called enlightenment because he has this awareness. So how could people be God when people change, but God does not change?[37]

Although we humans do change, God never changes. His characteristics, including His love for us, are constant and enduring.

We have excellent reasons to trust in Jesus rather than trusting in ourselves. Pantheism may have a growing fan base and offer many appealing ideas, but its logic is flawed, its promises are empty, and it offers no real power to change a person's life for the better. Jesus Christ and His spiritual claims, on the other hand, have stood the tests of time.

Jesus' promises are found to be true by those who dare to take Him at His word and trust in Him. Then, to top it off, He doesn't just expect us to strive hard to become better people; He offers us power from heaven through the Holy Spirit. By means of the Spirit, those who trust in Jesus are filled with a God-given ability and inner strength to live upright lives that please God and make a positive impact in the world.

Chapter Six

. . . .

Why Should I Trust Jesus When There is **So Much Disagreement** about the Identity of the "Real Jesus"?

"If anyone tries to flag you down, calling out, 'Here's the Messiah!' or points, 'There he is!' don't fall for it. Fake Messiahs and lying preachers are going to pop up everywhere. Their impressive credentials and dazzling performances will pull the wool over the eyes of even those who ought to know better. But I've given you fair warning."

—Jesus (Matthew 24:23–25 THE MESSAGE)

Our culture talks a lot about Jesus. I searched the word *Jesus* at Amazon.com and found more than 391,201 books about Jesus. These books are written from many different perspectives. As a result, we hear a lot of contradictory and confusing theories about who Jesus is.

For example, a university professor may talk about a "Jesus of history" that is not the same as the "Jesus of faith" described in the Bible. My Muslim friends in high school talked about Jesus, as did my Mormon friends, and yet their "Jesuses" seemed quite different from the One I have come to know. Even in Hollywood, some movie stars wear T-shirts that declare, "Jesus is my homeboy."

As Mark Driscoll, a pastor from Seattle, observes, "Musically, everyone, from rapper Kanye West to rockers The Killers, punk rockers Green Day, American Idol country-crooner Carrie Underwood, and the world's top band, U2, [is] singing about Jesus."[1] So is musician Kid Rock, who sings on one of his albums, "I'm gonna save your soul; it's really what you want me to do; Get on your knees; I'm your rock-n-roll Jesus."[2]

Other musicians and celebrities have made it a point to let us know that they aren't very impressed with Jesus. John Lennon of the Beatles once said:

> Christianity will go. It will vanish and shrink. I needn't argue with that; I'm right and I will be proved right. We're more popular than Jesus now: I don't know which will go first— rock and roll or Christianity.[3]

While some people find it fashionable to talk about Jesus, others are turned off by the mere mention of His name. In the Comedy Central series *South Park*, Jesus is characterized in one of the episodes as a council member in "Imaginationland," along with truly fictional characters such as Morpheus from *The Matrix* and Popeye. By depicting Jesus in this way, *South Park* is implying that Jesus is only a legend, a fabricated character.

Philosopher Bertrand Russell brazenly said, "Historically, it is quite doubtful whether Christ has existed. And if he did, we know nothing of him at all."[4] Friedrich Nietzsche, the influential existentialist philosopher said, "Jesus is an idiot,"[5] and "I condemn Christianity."[6]

In a contemporary response to comments like these, Christian author Josh McDowell asked the question, "Why is it that you can talk about God and nobody gets upset, but as soon as you mention Jesus, people often want to stop the conversation? Why have men and women down through the ages been divided over the question, 'Who is Jesus?'"[7] McDowell continues:

Almost 2,000 years ago, Jesus entered the human race in a small Jewish community. He was a member of a poor family, a minority group, and resided in one of the smallest countries in the world. He lived approximately thirty-three years, of which only the last three comprised his public ministry. Yet people almost everywhere still remember him. The date of our morning newspaper or the copyright date of a university textbook bears witness to the fact that Jesus lived one of the greatest lives ever lived.

WHAT ABOUT THE JESUS OF THE "OTHER GOSPELS"?

In 1945, archeologists discovered several documents in Nag Hammadi, Egypt (near Cairo), that are now known as the Nag Hammadi, or Gnostic gospels. The people who authored these books in the first several centuries after Christ's birth belonged to a variety of groups known as Gnostics, because they claimed to have *gnosis,* or "secret knowledge," about God.

Gnosticism consisted of a bizarre blend of neo-Christianity, Babylonian astrology, Neo-Platonism, mysticism, and magic. Some scholars believe that Gnosticism had roots in a heretical sect of Judaism. Many of the earliest theologians believed that Simon the Sorcerer from Samaria (see Acts 8) was the founder of Gnosticism. These early church fathers, including Irenaeus, Justin Martyr, Clement of Alexandria, and Tertullian, refuted the Gnostics and their claims to have special knowledge.[8]

I once assigned my high school theology and philosophy students to read *The Gospel of Thomas.* I wanted them to be prepared to enter a college classroom and hear their agnostic religion professor, who might have a PhD from a respected Ivy League school, tell them how the Gnostic Jesus is more beautiful, tolerant, and historically accurate than the New Testament Jesus. I wanted my students to be able to recognize for themselves that the Gnostic gospels not only borrow from the New Testament Gospels, but they also add some wacky sayings. For example, *The Gospel of Thomas* records Jesus as saying:

> "Blessed is the lion which becomes man when consumed by man; and cursed is the man whom the lion consumes, and the lion becomes man."[9]

My students' initial thoughts were like yours and mine: *What are they thinking? This makes absolutely no sense!* Of course, a proponent of Gnosticism might tell us that the reason we don't understand this saying is because we don't have *gnosis*, we haven't been illuminated.

Some liberal and feminist theologians say they appreciate the elevated role women play in the Gnostic gospels. I find that ironic, considering that a simple reading of these documents makes it clear that the status of women is higher in the New Testament Gospels. Consider this example from *The Gospel of Thomas*:

> Simon Peter said to them, "Let Mary leave us, for women are not worthy of life."
>
> Jesus said, "I myself shall lead her in order to make her male, so that she too may become a living spirit resembling you males. For every woman who will make herself male will enter the kingdom of heaven."[10]

What?! Why would any woman want Jesus to make her male? I guess she would have to have *gnosis* to understand! As you can see for yourself, this gospel is neither complimentary nor tolerant of women and their status. By contrast, the New Testament gospels portray Jesus as treating women with grace, honor, respect, true love, and purity.

Even though we find many false sayings in the Gnostic Gospels, we also find some true statements. For example, they acknowledge that Jesus Christ lived in history. Nevertheless, we can pinpoint three basic reasons why most scholars will not place these gospels on the same level as the biblical Gospels.

First, the biblical Gospels were written by Jesus' disciples and close associates in the first century. The biblical authors were either eyewitnesses of Christ's bodily resurrection or were close associates of the apostles who were eyewitnesses. The Gnostic gospels, however, were not written by the apostles; they were written by second-and-third century Gnostic teachers. Some Gnostic authors believed that they became "possessed" by a mystical spirit or the special knowledge of Thomas, Peter, Judas, or some other Christ-follower. But they were not eyewitnesses, and they had not received their information from eyewitnesses. The early church rejected their claims because Thomas, Peter, and Judas had been dead for years (sometimes hundreds of years) before these books were written.

Second, the biblical Gospels were widely distributed and almost universally accepted as authentic and authoritative by the early church leaders. The early church did not *determine* which books would go into the Bible. Ultimately God had already determined in His sovereignty which books would be included in His Word and inspired the apostles to write the Scriptures. Yet even though it was God, not the church, who determined the books that make up the Bible, the church *discovered* which books were authoritative by the approval of the apostles.

The authors of the New Testament Gospels backed up their claims of apostleship by being witnesses of Christ and also by performing extraordinary miracles in front of multitudes of eyewitnesses. We only have a few manuscripts of the Gnostic gospels, but we have over five thousand Greek manuscripts of the New Testament Gospels.

Third, the "other gospels" contain unorthodox doctrines and strange teachings. Some of the Gnostic gospels consider the resurrection of Christ to be simply spiritual, not physical or literal. And many of the teachings, as we have already mentioned, are quite bizarre. For instance, *The Gospel of Peter* claims that a huge talking cross came from the tomb at Christ's resurrection. In *The Infancy Gospel of Thomas,* Christ causes sickness and even kills some people in order to heal and resurrect them. If any seeker of the truth wants to compare the Christ of the Bible to the Christ of the Gnostics, simply read the four biblical Gospels, and then read the other gospels. It is clear that the Jesus of the Gnostic gospels does not mesh at all with what we know about the real Jesus.

How Can We Know the Identity of the Real Jesus?

We need not be confused; we have adequate evidence to know the identity of the real Jesus. In any controversy or court case, the more good evidence is presented, the more likely it is that the truth of the matter will be determined. Harvard professor Simon Greenleaf, the best authority on the law of evidence in the nineteenth century, said, "All that Christianity asks of men on this subject is (that the testimony of the Gospels) be sifted as if it were given in a court of justice."[11] Here are three sources of good evidence—clear indicators of who Jesus really was.

First, we have good evidence about Jesus from what early non-Christians said about Him. Flavius Josephus (circa AD 37–100), the most prolific Jewish historian of the first century, worked for the Roman emperor Domitian as a professional historian. Josephus recorded major historical events, including the destruction of Jerusalem in AD 70, and authored several major works, including *Antiquities of the Jews,* which was completed in AD 93. Josephus, who was not a Christian, wrote:

> At this time there was a wise man who was called Jesus. And his conduct was good, and he was known to be virtuous. Many people from among the Jews and other nations became his disciples. Pilate condemned him to be crucified and to die. And those who had become his disciples did not abandon his discipleship. They reported that he had appeared to

them three days after his crucifixion and that he was alive; accordingly, he was perhaps the Messiah concerning whom the prophets have recounted wonders.[12]

Michael Wilkins and J. P. Moreland conclude that, even if we did not have any Christian writings like those of the apostles and early church fathers, "we would be able to conclude from such non-Christian writings as Josephus, the *Talmud,* Tacitus, and Pliny the Younger that:

- Jesus was a Jewish teacher.
- Many people believed that he performed healings and exorcisms.
- He was rejected by the Jewish leaders.
- He was crucified under Pontius Pilate in the reign of Tiberius.
- Despite this shameful death, his followers, who believed that he was still alive, spread beyond Palestine so that there were multitudes of them in Rome by AD 64.
- All kinds of people from the cities and countryside—men and women, rich and poor, slave and free—worshiped him as God by the beginning of the second century.[13]

Dr. Norman Geisler and Frank Turek have noted:

Including Josephus, there are ten known non-Christian writers who mention Jesus within 150 years of his life. By contrast, over the same 150 years, there are nine non-Christian sources who mention Tiberius Caesar, the Roman emperor at the time of Jesus. So discounting all the Christian sources, Jesus is actually mentioned by one more source than the Roman emperor. If you include the Christian sources, authors mentioning Jesus outnumbered those who mentioned Tiberius 43 to 10![14]

Second, we have good evidence about the life of Jesus from personal eyewitness accounts of His life, death, and resurrection. One of the reasons that we can trust the New Testament writers, as was mentioned before, is that they were either apostles who were eyewitnesses or they gathered information from apostles who were eyewitnesses. Both Matthew and John were among Jesus' twelve close disciples. Most scholars believe that Mark wrote the words of Peter, one of Jesus' three closest disciples. The apostle Paul was closely connected with the first Christians, actively persecuting those early followers of Christ until he had a supernatural revelation of Jesus himself. Luke was not an apostle, but he was a close companion of Paul. Luke, who was a medical doctor with a scientific background, clearly states that he thoroughly and carefully investigated the facts and claims of Christ before writing his gospel.[15]

The Bible was written by at least forty authors, who wrote the books over a span of sixteen hundred years. God chose these authors from every walk of life: they were kings, peasants, philosophers, fishermen, poets, scholars, and statesmen. Nevertheless, together these writers presented a unified portrait of Jesus Christ:

- He was born in humble circumstances in the land of Israel.
- He was a real man who had typical daily responsibilities as a carpenter.
- He was God in the flesh, the perfect demonstration of God to mankind.
- He was sinless and served as the perfect sacrifice for man's sinful condition.
- He suffered a horrible death on the cross but rose again, conquering death and making the way for eternal life to all who will believe in Him.

The New Testament authors were quite aware of myths and aberrant teachings about Jesus that were floating around. So they emphasized to their readers that the events recorded in their writings really did happen.

- Simon Peter said, "We did not follow cleverly invented stories when we told you about the power and coming of our Lord Jesus Christ, but we were eyewitnesses of his majesty."[16]
- The apostle John wrote about a Jesus who was not just some spirit being or mystical concept; John wrote about a real flesh-and-blood person who was both soul and body, and had died and resurrected. "That which was from the beginning, which we have heard, which we have seen with our eyes, which we have looked at and our hands have touched—this we proclaim concerning the Word of life. The life appeared; we have seen it and testify to it, and we proclaim to you the eternal life, which was with the Father and has appeared to us."[17]
- Luke wrote about Jesus' death, "God raised this Jesus to life, and we are all witnesses of the fact."[18]
- The apostle Paul declared that Jesus was seen after His resurrection by His disciples and "more than five hundred of the brothers at the same time, most of whom are still living, though some have fallen asleep."[19]

The eyewitness accounts about Jesus are reliable and abundant; they can certainly help us know who the real Jesus is.

Third, we have good evidence about Jesus from multiple, specific, and fulfilled prophecies of a coming Messiah. Suppose you received an e-mail from a prospective business client whom you have never met before. He wants you to meet him at a coffee shop in Dallas, Texas, at 8:30 on Tuesday morning, March 3. You might ask, "Which coffee shop?"

Your associate might suggest, "How about a Starbucks?"

Well, there are hundreds of Starbucks in Dallas. So you ask, "Which one?"

"3216 Knox Street near Highland Park," responds your associate. *That Starbucks is always crowded,* you think to yourself. Then you ask, "How will I recognize you?"

"I'll be working on an Apple notebook and will be wearing glasses."

Many people at Starbucks have an Apple notebook and wear glasses. "What do you look like?" you ask.

"I'm six feet and seven inches tall with blond hair."

You laugh. "Not too many people are that tall! I should have no problem finding you."

Your associate adds, "By the way, I'll be wearing a bright red tie!"

Bet you won't miss him with all of those details!

Based on the multitude of specific details (the city, the time, the location, physical description, and so on), you are reasonably confident that you will be able to locate your associate. If he shows up on time, you will consider his description of the meeting place trustworthy.

Hundreds of years before Christ came, God gave us specific details through prophecy so that we would know exactly who His Son was and so we could trust Him. He wanted to help us recognize Christ and know that He was the Messiah.

Adapted from Josh McDowell's *Beyond Belief to Convictions,*[20] the following is a list of other messianic prophecies in the Hebrew Scriptures. God said the Messiah would be in:

- The nation of Israel, a descendant of Abraham (Genesis 22:18; Gal. 3:16).
- The lineage of Isaac (Genesis 21:12; Luke 3:23–24).
- The line of Jacob (Numbers 24:17; Luke 3:23–24).
- The tribe of Judah (Genesis 49:10; Luke 3:22–23).
- The family of Jesse (Isaiah 11:1; Luke 3:23–32).
- The house of David (Jeremiah 23:5; Luke 3:23–31).

Through the prophet Micah, God even gave the name of Jesus' specific place of birth: Bethlehem, a tiny town in the region of Judah (Micah 5:2; Matthew 2:1).

Through the book of Psalms and the prophet Isaiah, God made specific comments about the uniqueness of His Son. He said:

- He will be preceded by a messenger who will prepare the way and announce His advent (Isaiah 40:3; Matt. 3:1–2).
- He will begin His ministry in Galilee (Isaiah 9:1; Matt. 4:12–17).
- He will teach in parables (Psalm 78:2; Matt. 13:34–35).
- He will perform miracles (Isaiah 35:5–6; Matt. 9:35).
- He will ride into the city of Jerusalem on a donkey (Zech. 9:9).
- He will have a zeal for purity in the temple (Psalm 69:9).

God wanted us to trust in Jesus, His Son, so much that in one twenty-four-hour time period, at least two dozen specific prophecies were fulfilled in Him—all spoken at least four hundred years before his birth!

1. He will be betrayed by a friend (Psalm 41:9; Matt. 26:48–49).
2. The price of His betrayal will be thirty pieces of silver (Zech. 11:12; Matt. 26:15).
3. His betrayal money will be cast to the floor of the temple (Zech. 11:13; Matt. 27:5).
4. The betrayal money will be used to buy the potter's field (Zech. 11:13; Matt. 27:27).
5. He will be forsaken and deserted by His disciples (Zech. 13:7; Mark 14:50).
6. He will be accused of by false witnesses (Psalm 35:11; Matt. 26:59–60).

7. He will be silent before His accusers (Isaiah 53:7; Matt. 27:12).

8. He will be wounded and bruised (Isaiah 53:5; Matt. 27:26).

9. He will be hated without cause (Psalm 69:4; John 15:25).

10. He will be mocked, ridiculed, and rejected (Isaiah 53:3; Matt. 27:27–31; John 7:5, 48).

11. He will collapse from weakness (Psalm 109:24–25; Luke 23:26).

12. He will be taunted (Psalm 22:6–8; Matthew 27:39–43).

13. People will shake their heads at Him (Psalm 22:6–8; Matt. 27:39).

14. People will stare at Him (Psalm 22:17; Luke 23:35).

15. He will be executed among "sinners" (Isaiah 53:12; Matt. 27:38).

16. His hand and feet will be pierced (Psalm 22:16; Luke 23:33).

17. He will pray for His persecutors (Isaiah 53:12; Luke 23:34).

18. His garments will be divided by the casting of lots (Psalm 22:18; John 19:23–24).

19. He will thirst (Psalm 69:21; John 19:28).

20. His bones will be left unbroken (Psalm 34:20; John 19:33).

21. His heart will rupture (Psalm 22:14; John 19:34).

22. His side will be pierced (Zech. 12:10; John 19:34).

23. Darkness will come over the land at midday (Amos 8:9; Matt. 27:45).

24. He will be buried in a rich man's tomb (Isaiah 53:9; Matt. 27:57–60).[21]

In the early spring of 1947, a young Bedouin shepherd boy was keeping an eye on his sheep one mile west of the north end of the Dead Sea, just about seven miles south of Jericho. After throwing a stone at a stray goat in the Judean desert, he heard the sound of breaking pottery. As first, he was a bit scared, wondering if he had heard a ghost.

The next day, the young shepherd returned with his cousins and entered a cave that had been untouched for generations. They found jars filled with what appeared to be leather. The young shepherd thought perhaps he could make some money by selling the nice leather to be used for shoes. He took his discovery to a shoe salesman, who happened to be an antiquities dealer on the side. The antiquities dealer, after observing the leather, recognized that there were four scrolls inside the protective leather, and he purchased the scrolls.

The dealer then turned around and sold the scrolls to an orthodox archbishop for about $250. After going through a couple of owners, the scrolls were purchased for $250,000. These Dead Sea Scrolls are now considered one of the greatest archeological discoveries of all time. One of these Dead Sea Scrolls includes a copy of the entire book (sixty-six chapters) of Isaiah that dates back to 100 BC (yes, that's "Before Christ," emphasizing the prophetical nature of the book). The scroll is twenty-four feet long and is the oldest biblical scroll that has ever been discovered. It is now protected in a vault in Jerusalem, and high-resolution images are available online for public examination. In this ancient Hebrew translation of Isaiah is a prophecy that has convinced many Jews to place their trust in Yeshua (the Hebrew spelling of Jesus):

> He grew up before him like a tender shoot,
>> and like a root out of dry ground.
>> He had no beauty or majesty to attract us to him,
>> nothing in his appearance that we should desire him.
> He was despised and rejected by men,
>> a man of sorrows, and familiar with suffering.
>> Like one from whom men hide their faces
>> he was despised, and we esteemed him not.

Surely he took up our infirmities
  and carried our sorrows,
    yet we considered him stricken by God,
    smitten by him, and afflicted.
But he was pierced for our transgressions,
  he was crushed for our iniquities;
    the punishment that brought us peace was upon him,
    and by his wounds we are healed.
We all, like sheep, have gone astray,
  each of us has turned to his own way;
    and the Lord has laid on him
    the iniquity of us all.
He was oppressed and afflicted,
   yet he did not open his mouth;
    he was led like a lamb to the slaughter,
    and as a sheep before her shearers is silent,
    so he did not open his mouth.
By oppression and judgment he was taken away.
   And who can speak of his descendants?
    For he was cut off from the land of the living;
    for the transgression of my people he was stricken.
He was assigned a grave with the wicked,
  and with the rich in his death,
    though he had done no violence,
    nor was any deceit in his mouth.
Yet it was the Lord's will to crush him and cause him to suffer,
  and though the Lord makes his life a guilt offering,
    he will see his offspring and prolong his days,
    and the will of the Lord will prosper in his hand.
After the suffering of his soul,
  he will see the light of life and be satisfied;
    by his knowledge my righteous servant will justify many,
    and he will bear their iniquities.

Therefore I will give him a portion among the great,
    and he will divide the spoils with the strong,
    because he poured out his life unto death,
    and was numbered with the transgressors.
For he bore the sin of many,
    and made intercession for the transgressors.[22]

Dr. Michael L. Brown grew up in a Jewish family and later placed his trust in Jesus. As a student, he investigated Hebrew prophecy, which led him to earn his PhD in Near Eastern languages and literatures from New York University. In an interview with Lee Strobel, Brown comments on this passage from Isaiah 52–53. "It's almost as if God said, 'I want to make it so absolutely clear Yeshua is the Messiah and that it's undeniable,'"[23] Brown said. "I almost feel as if God would have to apologize to the human race and to the Jewish people for putting this passage into the Scriptures, when it so clearly points to Yeshua, if He didn't really mean that."[24]

Clearly, God meant to refer to Jesus in these passages. Without a doubt, He wanted you and me to know who His Son was, and because of all of this overwhelming archeological and historical evidence, we can trust Him. Just like Dr. Brown and others who have placed their trust in the Suffering Servant, we should, too. Jesus, the Servant, was pierced for our transgressions and carried our sorrows. He sacrificed Himself for us, and He rose again to give us eternal life. This is the Jesus of the Bible and the Jesus of history. And because of this, we can trust Him fully.

Chapter Seven

Why Should I Trust Jesus More Than Any Other Spiritual Leader?

*"At the name of Jesus every knee should bow,
in heaven and on earth and under the earth,
and every tongue confess that Jesus Christ
is Lord, to the glory of God the Father."*

—Philippians 2:10–11

The other day, I picked up the phone and called up a friend of mine who is a student at Harvard to see how he was doing. I asked for permission to share his fascinating life story with you. Playing the role of a journalist, I asked Abdoul, "Are you still trusting Jesus?"

Abdoul responded without hesitation: "Yes."

"Why?" I asked. "After everything you've been through, especially in the last several years, why do you still trust Jesus?"

"I trust Him because of His atonement on the cross. Jesus died for my sins, and sinful people need the blood of Jesus."

I wanted to hear more. Many Christians might have responded with a similar answer. But when Abdoul talks about the blood of Jesus, I get the feeling that his trust in Jesus is not just a part of his life; it is essential, his greatest hope.

Abdoul was born in Burkina Faso, West Africa, and grew up a devout Muslim, the son of an influential imam (Islamic spiritual leader). For the majority of Abdoul's life, he trusted Allah and his prophet Mohammed. Abdoul devoutly memorized the Quran and journeyed to Mecca on several occasions to worship Allah in the holy city. As a student at a leading academic institution, Abdoul has a sharp mind and knows several languages.

Abdoul moved to the United States a few years ago to pursue his education. He excelled academically despite his minimal knowledge of English. During his time in the United States, Abdoul's spiritual life has been greatly affected in ways that he and his father did not expect.

After living a couple of years in the United States, Abdoul met a banker named Larry. Over time, Larry, a recent convert to Christianity himself, befriended Abdoul and began to share his faith with him. Larry encouraged Abdoul to read the Bible.

Through Larry's friendship and by evaluating the accounts of Christ in the gospels of Matthew, Mark, Luke, and John, Abdoul was drawn to the love and compassion of Jesus. Abdoul examined the New Testament texts to see if they were reliable. After making a thorough investigation, Abdoul was moved by the historical resurrection of Christ, as well the number of eyewitnesses of Jesus and the detailed documentation recorded by Luke, the physician. On Easter Sunday 2002, in Atlanta, Georgia, Abdoul began to trust Jesus Christ with his life.

"Abdoul," I said, "there is a message that I hear some Christian teachers promote on television—that if you just have enough faith and trust in Jesus, you won't have to suffer; you can just claim health and wealth, and because you are a child of God, He has to give it to you. The message says that 'trusting Jesus' is better than any other religion, because you won't have as many struggles and you will be richer. Has that been the case for you? Since trusting Jesus in 2002, has life been completely easy?"

"No," Abdoul responded. "My father is an imam in Burkina

Faso. Islam teaches that if a Muslim becomes a Christian, then he must be excommunicated. He is also kicked out of the family. If you refuse to repent and turn back to Islam, you will be killed. When I became a Christian, my father threatened to murder me. My mother did not appreciate the way my father was threatening me, so she stood up for me to my father. In 2004, my father beat her to death."

From the tone of Abdoul's voice, it was obvious that the horrible memories and deep pain were still fresh in his mind.

Not wanting to linger on the topic of his mother's death, Abdoul continued. "Soon after my conversion, my father sent my younger brother to study at one of the top Islamic schools in Cairo, Egypt. He wanted my brother to convert me back to Islam. But I had enrolled in seminary, and I challenged my brother to look at the historical reliability of the life of Christ and the apostle Paul. My brother took some time to study and travel to several places, including Israel. Through many hours of research and careful investigation, he became convinced that the Christ of the Bible was true and the Quran was not historically accurate. He went back to the university to tell his friends about reliability of the Christ and the New Testament. Two days later, his dead body was discovered in his apartment, riddled with bullets and covered in blood."

As Abdoul told me about this mind-numbing tragedy, my thoughts flashed back to a time several years ago when I was eating lunch with Abdoul after his brother's murder. Abdoul's agony and sorrow were apparent, but it was also clear that Abdoul had not given up his trust in God. In fact, it seemed that his trust in Jesus was actually growing stronger. In the months following the deaths of his mother and brother, Abdoul had opportunities to share his testimony at some of the greatest academic institutions and the largest churches in the United States. Abdoul also raised money to help fund a school in his home village in Burkina Faso.

Shortly thereafter, Abdoul told me that his father's heart was finally beginning to soften. God was working in Abdoul's life, even though he and his relatives were paying a dear price for abandoning

Islam and trusting in Jesus Christ for salvation.

Abdoul will be the first to tell you that being a Christian is an incredible blessing. But it is not always easy. He admits that he got so busy doing ministry at one point that his family life greatly suffered. Abdoul has decided to pursue a career in politics and government, and since then, he has faced even more spiritual struggles in his life. God has an amazing plan for Abdoul's life, and Satan and his forces of evil want to keep Abdoul from bringing that plan to fruition.

Trusting Jesus is not trouble free for any of us. In fact, Jesus warned His followers, "No servant is greater than his master. If they persecuted me, they will persecute you also."[1] He also told them, "Whoever doesn't take up his cross and follow Me is not worthy of Me. Anyone finding his life will lose it, and anyone losing his life because of Me will find it."[2]

I asked Abdoul, "Now that you are preparing to pursue your master's degree, what helps you to trust Jesus at such a prestigious institution as Harvard?"

"I talk with friends like you," Abdoul said. "I read the Bible every day and pray."

"Is it arrogant for a Christian to say that Jesus is better than Mohammed or any other prophet or spiritual leader?" I asked.

"No, I don't think it's arrogant."

"Then tell me, Abdoul, what makes Jesus better? Specifically, as a former Muslim, why do you think that Jesus is better than Mohammed?"

Abdoul replied tenderly, "Jesus did not come as a warrior. He didn't kill people. He helped the poor. He tried to resolve issues peacefully without war. He told His followers to lay down their weapons."

"Like Jesus did in Gethsemane with Peter?" I asked.

"Yes. Jesus loved people and won them over not with weapons, but through His love."

As we ended our conversation, I asked Abdoul, "What are some practical things that we Christians really need to work on?"

"We need to know the Bible and defend the Bible with love and respect," Abdoul responded. "We also need to reach people with the love of Christ."

Abdoul's story of conversion and persecution reveals that this former Muslim has sound reasons for trusting Jesus more than any other religious leader. We should not trust Jesus because we think He's going to make life easy for us, or because we hope He'll make us healthy and wealthy. We trust Jesus because of who He is—His deity and humanity, His atoning death on the cross, and His demonstration of love.

Jesus' atoning death on the cross separates Him from Mohammed, Buddha, Moses, Abraham, Gandhi, and every other spiritual leader. Christ's blood shed on the cross was the atonement for the sins of every man and woman on earth. The prophet John understood Christ's mission on earth when he saw Jesus and said, "Behold! the Lamb of God who takes away the sins of the world!"[3] For our sins to be forgiven, Christ, who is fully God and fully man, had to take the punishment and wrath of God the Father on the cross.

I'd like to dispel one misconception: it wasn't just the Jews who were responsible for the death of Christ. The Romans were also responsible. And so are you. And so am I. He died for *our* sins. Yet Jesus also said, "No one takes [my life] from me, but I lay it down of my own accord."[4] In other words, God chose for this to happen. Jesus knew the plan, and He willingly and obediently laid down His life for us.[5]

Even though God is loving, He is also holy and just. Because He is holy, He must be separated from sin. But why crucify Christ? He was an innocent man! Even His enemies, like Pilate, repeatedly said, "I find no fault in this man."[6] It may seem unjust for God the Father to prearrange the death of His Son. Yet it was God's incredible love for you and me—in the midst of all our sins—that motivated this ultimate, sacrificial act. Scripture says, "Very rarely will anyone die for a righteous man, though for a good man someone might possibly dare to die. But God demonstrates his own love for us in this: While we were still sinners, Christ died for us."[7]

When Christ hung on that cross, He took on all the sins of the whole world. God's wrath demanded a perfect sacrifice. But only God is perfect. Therefore, God had to die on the cross. Yet the sacrifice had to be human, as well. Why? We are humans, and every human has a sinful nature that falls short of God's perfect standard. Jesus is unique because He alone is fully human and yet fully God—and God is perfect. No other religious leader has ever made such claims as Jesus. Most religious leaders tell us, "I will show you the way." But Jesus said, "*I am* the way . . . No one comes to the Father except through me."[8] This is the ultimate reason we can trust Jesus more than any other spiritual leader—because of who He is.

JESUS IS FULLY GOD

Let's consider two distinct, yet complementary truths. Jesus is both fully God and fully man. Ever since Jesus walked this earth, many critics have denied that Jesus is God. In the New Testament, some skeptics said, "He's demon possessed."[9] Others mocked, "He is a glutton and a drunkard."[10] But most people are not so derogatory. Most people will acknowledge that Christ was a historical person, not just a legend. Many say positive things about Him. Yet they still deny that He is God.

In the fourth century, a theologian named Arius denied the full deity of Jesus. His followers where known as Arians. He taught that Christ possessed a nature that was similar to that of God the Father, but not the same. Arius' claims were refuted theologically by Athanasius, who defended the doctrinal position of "Christ being fully human and fully divine." Unfortunately, the subtle attacks of Arius continue today. For example, the character Leigh Teabing in Dan Brown's novel *The Da Vinci Code* claims that it was Constantine who "promoted" Christ's status to deity at the Council of Nicea.[11]

This is a ridiculous claim. The majority of Christ's earliest followers understood Jesus to be both a man and the Messiah, the Son of God.[12] Peter called Jesus, "the Christ, the Son of the living God."[13] After His resurrection, the disciple Thomas called Him, "my Lord and my God."[14] Paul said, "In Christ all the fullness of the Deity lives in bodily form."[15] The writer of Hebrews says about Jesus, "Your throne, O God, will last for ever."[16] Followers of Christ who lived after the New Testament writers still considered Jesus to be God. In AD 105, Ignatius said, "God Himself was manifested in human form."[17] In AD 150, the church father Clement said, "It is fitting that you should think of Jesus Christ as God."[18]

Some opponents of Christianity make another objection to the idea that Jesus was divine. They assert that Jesus never claimed to be divine, or the Messiah, or God incarnate. The following examples clearly refute such thinking.

Jesus claimed to be the great "I AM."

During Moses' miraculous encounter with God at the burning bush on Mount Horeb, God spoke to Moses in an audible voice. He told him he knew about the misery of His people, and that Moses was to tell Pharaoh to "let my people go."

> Moses responded to God and said, "What's your name?"
> God said, to Moses, "I AM who I AM. This is what you are to say to the Israelites: 'I AM has sent me to you.'"[19]

Two thousand years later, when Jesus was questioned about His identity, He applied that very same name for God to Himself:

> At this the Jews exclaimed, "Now we know that you are demon-possessed! Abraham died and so did the prophets, yet you say that if anyone keeps your word, he will never taste death. Are you greater than our father Abraham? He died, and so did the prophets. Who do you think you are?"
> Jesus replied, "If I glorify myself, my glory means noth-

ing. My Father, whom you claim as your God, is the one who glorifies me. Though you do not know him, I know him. If I said I did not, I would be a liar like you, but I do know him and keep his word. Your father Abraham rejoiced at the thought of seeing my day; he saw it and was glad."

"You are not yet fifty years old," the Jews said to him, "and you have seen Abraham!"

"I tell you the truth," Jesus answered, "before Abraham was born, I am!" At this, they picked up stones to stone him, but Jesus hid himself, slipping away from the temple grounds.[20]

The Jews were already ticked off at Jesus when He started talking about having a special relationship with the Father. Once He claimed to be "I AM," they wanted to stone Him!

Jesus claimed equality with God the Father.

On several other occasions, Jesus made some rather bold statements about His equality with God the Father. In Mark's gospel, Jesus identified Himself as deity by claiming that He could forgive sins.[21] Everybody knew that only God is qualified to forgive sins! The religious leaders tried to stone Jesus because He was "calling God his own Father, making himself *equal* with God."[22]

Jesus claimed to be the "Son of Man."

In another part of Mark's gospel, Jesus claimed deity by calling Himself the "Son of Man," a popular Messianic term used by the prophet Daniel. Sometimes in the Old Testament, the expression "son of man" is used for ordinary men.[23] However, the prophet Daniel made a specific prophecy about a Son of Man who would have the authority of God and who would receive worship. This Son of Man would have to *be* God if people were to worship Him. "For it is written, 'Worship the Lord your God, and serve him only.'"[24] Daniel wrote:

In my vision at night I looked, and there before me was one
like a son of man, coming with the clouds of heaven. He
approached the Ancient of Days and was led into his presence. He was given authority, glory and sovereign power; all
peoples, nations and men of every language worshiped him.
His dominion is an everlasting dominion that will not pass
away, and his kingdom is one that will never be destroyed.[25]

Again the high priest asked him, "Are you the Christ, the Son
of the Blessed One?"

"I am," said Jesus. "And you will see the Son of Man sit-
ting at the right hand of the clouds of the Mighty One and
coming on the clouds of heaven.[26]

Notice that Jesus is claiming to be (1) the Messiah, (2) the Son
of the Blessed One, (3) the "I AM," (4) the Son of Man, and (5) the
One "coming with the clouds of heaven." Because of Christ's claims
to be God, look what happens next:

The high priest tore his clothes. "Why do we need any more
witnesses?" he asked. "You have heard the blasphemy. What
do you think?"

They all condemned him as worthy of death. Then some
began to spit at him; they blindfolded him, struck him with
their fists, and said, "Prophesy!" And the guards took him
and beat him.[27]

In *Mere Christianity*, C. S. Lewis argues that since Jesus clearly
claimed to be God, there are only three possibilities regarding His
identity. Either He was a liar, a lunatic, or Lord. Liar doesn't fit the
facts. Jesus lived and taught the highest standard of ethics. And it's
unlikely that He would have laid down His life unless He really
thought He was telling the truth. And if He was a liar, then it doesn't
do to call Him a great moral teacher. Great moral teachers don't

deceive people by falsely claiming to be God.

If Jesus thought He was God, but really wasn't, then He would have been a lunatic. But "lunatic" doesn't fit Jesus either, for He was a clear-thinking man who uttered some of the most profound sayings ever recorded. And everyone—even His enemies—claimed that Jesus was a man of great integrity who taught the truth and worked extraordinary miracles.

Bono, the lead singer of U2, explained some of the same principles in a conversation with Michka Assayas.[28]

Assayas: Christ has his rank among the world's great thinkers. But Son of God, isn't that far-fetched?

Bono: No, it's not far-fetched to me. Look, the secular response to the Christ story always goes like this: He was a great prophet, obviously a very interesting guy, had a lot to say along the lines of the other great prophets, be they Elijah, Muhammad, Buddha, or Confucius. But actually Christ doesn't allow you that. He doesn't let you off that hook. Christ says, No. I'm not saying I'm a teacher, don't call me a teacher. I'm not saying I'm a prophet. I'm saying: I'm the Messiah. I'm saying: I am God incarnate. And people say: No, no, please just be a prophet. A prophet we can take. You're a bit eccentric. We've had John the Baptist eating locusts and wild honey, we can handle that. But don't mention the "M" word! Because, you know. We're gonna have to crucify you. And he goes: No, no, I know you're expecting me to come back with an army and set you free from these creeps, but actually I am the Messiah. At this point, everyone starts staring at their shoes, and says: Oh, man, he's gonna keep saying this. So what you're left with is either Christ was who He said He was—the Messiah—or a complete nutcase. I mean, we're talking nutcase on the level of Charles Manson

. . . I'm not joking here. The idea that the entire course of civilization for over half of the globe could have its fate changed and turned upside-down by a nutcase, for me that's far-fetched.

JESUS WAS FULLY HUMAN

In order for Christ to be the perfect substitution for you and me on the cross, He must have been fully God. In order for God the Father to accept His sacrifice, Jesus had to be a perfect and unblemished Lamb. He had to be God in the flesh. But He must also have been fully human. In order for Him to die in our place, He had to become human, because we are human.

Mark Driscoll, in his book *Vintage Jesus,* says this about the humanity of Christ:

Jesus was a dude. Like my drywaller dad, he was a construction worker who swung a hammer for a living. Because Jesus worked in a day when there were no power tools, he likely had calluses on his hands and muscles on his frame, and did not look like so many of the drag-queen Jesus images that portray him with long, flowing, feathered hair, perfect teeth, and soft skin, draped in a comfortable dress accessorized by matching open-toed sandals and handbag.[29]

Jesus was a real man in flesh. He:

- began His life as a real human baby born of a woman
- went through the developmental stages of childhood
- worked as a carpenter
- became hungry and thirsty
- became tired and fatigued
- experienced sadness and the death of His friend Lazarus (He wept)
- experienced gladness and was joyful

In all of these ways, Jesus revealed His humanity. Because He was eternal, Jesus was always God. But when Christ was conceived in the womb of Mary, He took on the nature of humanity. In this nature, He allowed Himself to be limited in knowledge. For example, when a woman in a crowd grabbed the hem of Jesus' garment, He felt power flow out of His body to heal her and asked, "Who touched my clothes?"[30] On another occasion, He told his disciples, "No one knows when the Son of Man is returning, only the Father." In His human nature, Jesus was limited in knowledge. Like most humans, He grew more intelligent and matured as He grew older (Luke 2:52).

However, as far as His God-nature was concerned, Jesus knew everything, even at birth. Jesus often knew everything about a person the first time He met them, as in the case of the Samaritan woman He met at the well (John 4). Jesus knew people's thoughts and understood their spiritual conditions, even when He had never met them.

It's almost impossible for us to comprehend the mystery of Christ having two natures. When the apostle Paul taught a young church at Philippi about this mystery, he explained that Christ had "emptied himself" of some of the glory that He enjoyed in heaven. Jesus chose to "give away" some of His privileges of deity while He lived on earth. Paul writes:

> Who, being in very nature God, did not consider equality with God something to be grasped, but made himself nothing, taking the very nature of a servant, being made in human likeness. And being found in appearance as a man, he humbled himself and became obedient to death—even death on a cross![31]

Paul said that because of Christ's humility, God has now exalted Him in heaven:

> Therefore God exalted him to the highest place and gave him the name that is above every name, that at the name of Jesus

every knee should bow, in heaven and on earth and under the earth, and every tongue confess that Jesus Christ is Lord, to the glory of God the Father.[32]

Historian Philip Schaff explains:

Jesus of Nazareth, without money and arms, conquered more millions than Alexander, Caesar, Mohammed, and Napoleon; without science and learning, He shed more light on things human and divine than all the philosophers and scholars combined; without the eloquence of schools, He spoke such words of life as were never spoken before or since, and produced effects which lie beyond the reach of the orator or poet; without writing a single line, He set more pens in motion, and furnished themes for more sermons, orations, discussions, learned volumes, works of art, and songs of praise, than the whole army of great men of ancient and modern times.[33]

THE BEAUTY OF CHRIST'S TWO NATURES

Jesus is the only founder of a religion we can trust, because He has gone through the same hardships we have, yet He never sinned. The eyewitness gospel accounts reveal that as Jesus was dying on the cross, He uttered a simple statement, which we ought to think about. Jesus said, "I am thirsty."[34] Author Max Lucado commented on this statement:

We see God the Son on a cross, lips cracked and mouth of cotton. Throat so dry, he can hardly swallow and voice so hoarse he could scarcely speak. But he says, "I am thirsty." Why did he allow himself to go so thirsty? Christ could have not been thirsty but still on the cross. Did he not cause jugs of water to be jugs of wine? Did he not make a wall out of the

Jordan River and two walls out of the Red Sea? Didn't he with one word banish the rain and calm the waves? Doesn't the Scripture say that he "turned the desert into pools" (Psalm 107:35) and "the hard rock into springs" (Psalm 114:8)? Did God not say, "I will pour water on him who is thirsty" (Isaiah 44:3)? If this is so, why does Jesus endure thirst? He came to die on a cross, not go thirsty.

While we are asking this question, add a few more. Why did Jesus grow weary in Samaria (John 4:6), disturbed in Nazareth (Mark 6:6), angry in the Temple (John 2:15)? Why was he sleepy in the boat on the Sea of Galilee (Mark 4:38), sad at the Tomb of Lazarus (John 11:35), and hungry in the wilderness (Matthew 4:2)?[35]

Why did Jesus endure all this? To identify with us in our frail human condition. God Almighty, through the person of Jesus Christ, knows our suffering and human experiences. Jesus has walked where we walk, so that "we do not have a high priest who is unable to sympathize with our weaknesses, but we have one who has been tempted in every way, just as we are—yet without sin."[36]

Have you ever had someone die whom you really cared about? Jesus wept at the death of His friend Lazarus. Have you ever had an authority figure jump all over your case when you did not think you deserved it—maybe a parent, a boss, a coach, or a teacher who falsely accused you? Jesus knows this experience, too. He was falsely accused by His parents as well as by religious leaders. As a twelve-year-old boy, He stayed behind in the temple teaching the Word of God to the religious leaders while His parents left the city. They didn't know He had stayed behind, so when they discovered that He was missing, they came back to find Him. And they were upset. "Why have you treated us like this?" they asked.[37] Jesus simply told them that they should have known that He would be in His Father's house. Jesus' parents had misjudged His motives.

Today some people struggle with anger and resentment over

what happened to them in their childhoods. Jesus' mother, Mary, was a godly woman, specially chosen by God to carry Jesus. Yet even she misunderstood Jesus in this case. But Christ did not resent His parents; He was always respectful of them. Maybe your parents have misunderstood you or accused you of impure motives. If so, Christ sympathizes with what you are feeling.

Have you ever felt forsaken, like you didn't have a single friend in the world? Jesus was denied and betrayed three times by one of His best friends, Peter. Another of His followers, Judas, handed Him over to be killed. Jesus had essentially been sold for a handful of silver pieces. So He has felt the pain of your rejection.

Scripture says, "He was despised and rejected by men, a man of sorrows, and familiar with suffering."[38] Jesus was even forsaken for a time by His own Father. God had to turn His back on the sins of the world when they fell upon Christ. On the cross, Jesus cried out, "My God, my God, why have you forsaken me?"[39] If you ever feel like God doesn't care about you, realize that Jesus understands. He feels what you are going through when you are tempted not to trust Him. The letter of Hebrews says this about Jesus:

> In all things He had to be made like His brethren, that He might become a merciful and faithful High Priest in things pertaining to God, to make propitiation for the sins of the people. For in that He Himself has suffered, being tempted, He is able to aid those who are tempted.[40]

We can trust Jesus because He alone is fully God as well as fully human. Unlike any other spiritual leader in all of human history, Jesus can be trusted because He has gone through the pain that you have experienced in life, yet without any sin. He loves you, and He is capable and qualified to meet your deepest needs.

Chapter Eight

Why Should I Trust Jesus in the Midst of **Suffering and Death?**

"The archeological discovery threatened to tear Western Civilization off its hinges. One out of every three people on the earth was affected—some 2,000,000,000 whose lives were suddenly, brutally wrenched out of joint. It was like waking up one morning to find that a week had ten days, that there were forty-three minutes in each hour, or that one counted, '1, 2, 8, 4, 5,' and—maddeningly—no one else thought anything amiss."

—from *A Skeleton in God's Closet*

These are some of the opening words from Dr. Paul Maier's bestselling novel, *A Skeleton in God's Closet*. In this exciting archeological thriller, Dr. Jonathan Weber, a Harvard professor and biblical theologian, joins a group of scholars on an archaeological dig in Israel. Their discovery is an archaeologist's dream come true. But it is also the worst nightmare for people of faith. In the novel, the scholars appear to have discovered the very bones of Jesus Christ of Nazareth. As the suspense builds, the reader realizes that this prospect threatens the very foundation of the Christian faith.[1]

I'm not a prophet, but let me make an easy prediction. This spring around Easter, some book or television special will come out that will try to deny the physical, bodily resurrection of Jesus Christ. It does not matter in which year you are reading this book. Critics of Christ's resurrection have always tried their best to come up with some explanation for the empty tomb and the transformed lives of the apostles.

In previous years, liberal scholars like John Dominic Crossan, Robert Greg Cavin, Barbara Thiering, and others have stated in interviews that the bodily resurrection of Jesus never took place. In March 2007, the Discovery Channel aired a show titled *The Lost Tomb of Jesus*, which was produced by Oscar-winning director James Cameron. The show's writers interviewed researchers about small baskets of bones that were discovered in Jerusalem, one of which bore the name, "Judas, the son of Jesus." Within a month of the show, the hype was over. No evidence was discovered that indicated that these bones were related to the Jesus of the Bible. Yet the show had sown many doubts in the hearts of viewers.

It can be tempting, in response to attempts to produce evidence that Christ did not rise from the dead, for Christians to say something like, "Whether the resurrection of Christ was physical or spiritual, it doesn't matter to me. My relationship with Jesus is personal, and I experience a spiritual relationship with Him through faith that is not based on historical facts."

In this chapter, I hope to demonstrate the error of this way of thinking. The basis of Christianity is not simply an "existential experience." The cornerstone of Christianity is not even faith *in itself*, although without faith it is impossible to please God.[2] The ultimate foundation of Christianity is a historical event: the bodily resurrection of Jesus Christ. A man who walked this earth in history claimed to be God, died on the cross, and physically rose from the dead. The apostle Paul said, "If Christ has not been raised from the dead, your faith is worthless; you are still in your sins. Therefore those who have fallen asleep in Christ have also perished. If we have placed our hope in Christ for this life only, we should be pitied more than anyone."[3]

In this chapter, as I reveal some of the historical evidence of the bodily resurrection of Christ, I will show the connection between the resurrection and its promises for overcoming suffering and death. The historical resurrection of Jesus Christ is a comfort in periods of grief. During difficult and tragic times of our lives when we feel that we can't even get out of bed in the morning, the resurrection of Christ gives us hope and a reason to live life each day with expectancy. Jesus came to die so that you may live abundantly. "Because I live," He said, "you also will live."[4]

As I have counseled families who have lost loved ones, I realized that many people who do not normally think about spirituality, heaven, or Jesus on a regular basis will think about the afterlife during times of grief and bereavement. The simple fact is that nobody likes funerals. They are the saddest times of our lives, times in which many people express their despair. Yet, I discovered that, even in the midst of such intense emotional suffering, family members who are not necessarily religious will begin to ask spiritual questions about the afterlife:

- Why did God allow this to happen?
- Where has my loved one gone?
- Will I see her again?
- Are our souls reincarnated into another person?
- What will heaven be like?
- If we are going to be raised up later, will our bodies be spiritual or physical?

Throughout history, philosophers and theologians have debated two specific questions: *What happens to one's soul after death?* and *What happens to one's body after death?* Perhaps these aren't the top two questions that come to your mind, but they are relevant to our daily lives. If you have a loved one who is slowly dying of cancer, you know that his or her body is decaying. It's not what it used to be. You want to have certainty that, for your friend or family member, wholeness and life and hope exist beyond the grave.

Throughout history, great thinkers have talked about life after death. Even though Socrates and Plato had confidence that the human soul lives on, their devout followers had no proof that their teaching was correct. In addition, most of these philosophers and spiritual teachers, though they spoke some truth, had a negative view of the physical body. Plato thought that the body was a prison the soul was anxiously waiting to escape—just like a bird trapped in a cage, desperately wanting to escape and soar through a bright blue sky.

Many philosophers, following the teachings of Greek pantheists and of Hindu leaders, not only have negative beliefs about the physical body, but also believe confidently in reincarnation. In fact, probably one third of the people in the world today believe in reincarnation, which is a theory that one's soul goes on to live in another body after death. This depressing view of the body exists amongst countless young adults throughout the world today. Often the human body is simply viewed as an object to be used and later cast aside.

EXTREME MAKEOVER?

As a teacher at an affluent Christian high school, I see some young female students who are starving themselves through eating disorders. They don't recognize that they are loved by God and beautiful in His sight. They don't realize that they are harming their bodies, the "temples" in which God resides through His Holy Spirit. Similarly, there are athletic teenage boys all across the country who use steroids to grow their muscles to run faster or jump higher. These young people are simply not satisfied with their bodies.

We are living in a culture in which most young adults, no matter how beautiful or handsome or athletic, want an "extreme makeover." Plastic surgery is growing in popularity. Surveys show that more than a third of American women are "strongly dissatis-fied with their bodies," and many other women are "somewhat dissatisfied."[5] Some depressed teens cut themselves because they believe that causing themselves physical pain will offer them relief from emotional pain. People of all walks of life believe that human bodies are simply objects to be lusted after and satisfied through the use of pornography and sexual sin.

Christianity opposes all of these degrading views of the human body. The apostle Paul called the human body the temple of the Holy Spirit.[6] Jesus taught His followers to love God with both soul (heart) and body (strength).

WHICH ONE IS TRUE?

As mentioned above, philosophers and theologians have won-dered for thousands of years which teacher knows the truth about life after death and how we can verify truth claims about the res-urrection of the body.

Mohammed spoke of the resurrection and paradise, but he never proved it. Buddha spoke of reincarnation, but we have no way to verify his claims because we can't observe the reincarnation of a soul. But over two thousand years ago, the Great Teacher—Jesus Christ—cleared up all confusion about the resurrection of the body. First, He taught that there will one day be a literal bodily res-urrection. He said, "Do not be amazed at this, for a time is coming when all who are in their graves will hear his voice and come out—those who have done good will rise to live, and those who have done evil will rise to be condemned."[7] The good news of Jesus is that, even though we die, our bodies will someday be raised again.

Moreover Jesus taught that your decision to be for Him or against Him will determine how that resurrection will take place. Those who have placed their faith in Jesus will be rewarded, and their bodies will be raised to spend eternity with Him; but those who have rejected Him will be condemned, and their bodies resurrected to live separated from Him in everlasting torment.

Finally, Jesus did not just espouse nice-sounding promises of an afterlife; He actually demonstrated the resurrection. Jesus reminded His followers over and over again that He was going to die and then be raised from the dead. After He died, Jesus certainly could have disposed of His first body—the one that was brutally flogged, crucified, and deeply scarred—and created another body for Himself, if He had wanted to. (He is God, after all.) But that's not what happened. It was the same body that was pierced and bruised and crucified that was physically resurrected three days later by God's mighty power. Christ bore the evidence of His suffering in His own body, which helped people who saw Him after the resurrection know that it was really Him they were seeing and not a ghost.

Couldn't Jesus have died and fulfilled the requirements of sacrificial atonement without a bodily resurrection? I suppose, hypothetically speaking, it was possible. But through the historical event of this physical resurrection, Jesus demonstrated victory over death.[8] Through His resurrection we can experience a new birth and have great hope for the future, no matter what pain and discomfort we experience in our physical bodies.[9] If Christ's body was severely beaten and torn for our sins and then raised in newness of life, then God certainly has the power to raise up our deteriorated and weakened bodies years after our death. It is comforting to remember this when a loved one passes away or a family member is diagnosed with a terminal illness. Through Christ's resurrection, we have been given the physical evidence of God's promise that a similar miracle will someday take place with our bodies.

Resurrection isn't difficult for God. If God had the power to create the universe out of nothing simply by His spoken word, then He certainly has the power to resurrect our created bodies as well. Because of the resurrection of Jesus Christ, we can face any physical difficulties and sorrows with the assurance that our bodies will be transformed supernaturally after death so that we can spend eternity with Him.

Evidence for the Historical Resurrection of Jesus

One of my college professors, Dr. Gary Habermas, has collected around 1,500 of the most scholarly works on the resurrection from 1975 to the present. As one of the leading experts on the resurrection, he has debated some of the most popular atheists. In *The Risen Jesus and Future Hope*, Habermas uses the "minimum facts" approach to argue that Jesus' resurrection was physical and historical. This approach leverages the evidence that virtually all scholars, from liberal agnostics and skeptical atheists to fundamentalist Christians, believe about the historical Jesus. Habermas argues that, regardless of theological conviction, virtually all scholars agree that the following statements about Jesus and His followers are historically true:

- Jesus died by Roman crucifixion.
- He was buried, most likely in a private tomb.
- Soon afterwards the disciples were discouraged, bereaved, and despondent, having lost hope.
- Jesus' tomb was found empty very soon after His interment.[10]
- The disciples had encounters with who they believed was the risen Jesus.
- Due to these experiences, the disciples' lives were thoroughly transformed. They were even willing to die for their belief.
- The proclamation of Christ's resurrection took place very early, from the beginning of church history.
- The disciples' public testimony and preaching of the resurrection took place in the city of Jerusalem, where Jesus had been crucified and buried shortly before.
- The earliest gospel message centered on the preaching of the death and resurrection of Jesus.

- Sunday, the day of Christ's resurrection, became the primary day for His followers to assemble and worship.
- James, the brother of Jesus and a skeptic before the resurrection, was converted because he also believed he saw the risen Jesus.
- Just a few years later, Saul of Tarsus (the apostle Paul) became a Christian after an encounter with what he believed was the risen Jesus.[11]

If we honestly consider these twelve points, we have great reason to trust Jesus. If all of these facts are accepted as true even by skeptics and atheists, then surely Jesus' resurrection is the greatest FEAT of all time.

The Greatest FEAT of All Time

Apologist Hank Hanegraaff has created an acronym to help us remember the greatest FEAT of all time: the resurrection of Jesus Christ.

> Fatal torment
> Empty tomb
> Appearances of Christ
> Transformation[12]

Fatal Torment

The letter F serves to remind us of Christ's "fatal torment"—the horrible suffering that led to His death. Hanegraaff writes, "We see that believing anything other than that Jesus suffered fatal torment takes more faith than the resurrection itself."[13] Even a liberal scholar of the Jesus Seminar, John Dominic Crossan, admits that the truth of Jesus' crucifixion "is as sure as anything historical can be."[14] The Romans were experts in execution. They made sure they got the job done, or they paid with their life. The March 21, 1986, issue of the *Journal of the American Medical Association* documented the impossibility that a victim could survive the Roman execution. The article concludes the following about Jesus:

> Jesus of Nazareth underwent Jewish and Roman trials, was flogged, and was sentenced to death by crucifixion. The scourging produced deep stripe-like lacerations and appreciable blood loss, and it probably set the stage for hypovolemic shock, as evidenced by the fact that Jesus was too weakened to carry the crossbar (patibulum) to Golgotha. At the site of crucifixion, his wrists were nailed to the patibulum and, after the patibulum was lifted onto the upright post (stipes), his feet were nailed to the stipes. The major pathophysiologic effect of crucifixion was an interference with normal respirations. Accordingly, death resulted primarily from hypovolemic shock and exhaustion asphyxia. Jesus' death was ensured by the thrust of a soldier's spear into his side. Modern medical interpretation of the historical evidence indicates that Jesus was dead when taken down from the cross.[15]

When you read the Scriptures, always remember that Jesus endured the fatal torment of the cross for you and me.

EMPTY TOMB

The E stands for "empty tomb." In a debate with Dr. Gerd Ludemann, Dr. William Lane Craig lists several pieces of evidence for the empty tomb:

- The empty tomb story is part of very old source material used by Mark.
- The old information transmitted by Paul in 1 Corinthians implies the fact of the empty tomb.

- The story is simple and lacks signs of legendary embellishment.
- The fact that women's testimony was worthless in first-century Palestine counts in favor of the women's role in discovering the tomb.[16]

In addition to Craig's comments, it seems that if the early Christians had fabricated a story about Jesus' resurrection, they would not have recorded the fact that all of the them fled after Jesus was taken captive by the Romans, while the brave and courageous women stayed with Him at the cross and were the first to show up at the empty tomb. If Peter had made up the story, he would not have allowed his friends Matthew and Mark to include the embarrassing details of his falling asleep the night that Jesus told him to "watch and pray." And he definitely wouldn't have allowed them to fabricate his threefold denial of Jesus.

APPEARANCES OF CHRIST

The A stands for "appearances of Christ." In another debate with John Dominic Crossan, Dr. William Lane Craig said, "On multiple occasions and under various circumstances, different individuals and groups of people experienced appearances of Jesus alive."[17] Many scholars are convinced that the following verses from 1 Corinthians 15 are actually an early creed about the resurrection that the early church recited when they gathered for weekly worship:

For I passed on you as most important what I also received:

that Christ died for our sins
    according to the Scriptures,
    that He was buried,
    that He was raised on the third day
    according to the Scriptures

and that He appeared to Cephas,
then to the Twelve.
then He appeared to over five hundred brothers at
one time,
most of whom remain to the present,
but some have fallen asleep.
Then He appeared to James, then to all the apostles.
Last of all, as to one abnormally born,
He also appeared to me.[18]

Craig says that this information is attested before AD 36.[19] Gary Habermas writes, "I'd agree with the various scholars who trace it back to within two to eight years of the Resurrection, or from about AD 32–38, when Paul received it either in Damascus or Jerusalem."[20] Paul said that Jesus appeared to over five hundred brothers at one time, but then added an important fact: "Most of whom remain to the present, but some have fallen asleep." In other words, Paul was saying that if you do not believe my testimony about the resurrection, then check it out with the eyewitnesses—hundreds of them are still alive.

TRANSFORMATION

The T stands for "transformation." When Jesus was arrested by the Roman guards, the disciples were terrified and fled for their lives. Peter denied Jesus three times that evening. A little servant girl approached Peter and said, "You look like one of his disciples." Peter, scared for his life, began to curse at her and said, "I don't know what you are talking about."

However, a few days later, something changed in Peter's life. He went from being a timid coward in front of a little servant girl to a bold witness, as he courageously stood in front of three thousand people and proclaimed the resurrection of Jesus. What happened? Peter saw a man who was dead come back to life! Here's what Peter preached on the day of Pentecost:

Men of Israel, listen to these words: This Jesus the Nazarene was a man pointed out to you by God with miracles, wonders, and signs that God did among you through Him, just as you yourselves know. Though He was delivered up according to God's determined plan and foreknowledge, you used lawless people to nail Him to a cross and kill Him. God raised Him up . . . God has resurrected this Jesus. We are witnesses of this . . . Repent . . . and be baptized, each of you, in the name of Jesus the Messiah for the forgiveness of your sins, and you will receive the gift of the Holy Spirit.[21]

Before the resurrection, James and Jude, the younger brothers of Jesus, did not believe that their older brother was really the Messiah. Jesus had not performed a miracle until He was in His thirties, when He turned the water into wine at a wedding party in Cana. Jesus probably lived a pretty normal life as a carpenter until He "revealed His glory." However, the lives of James and Jude were dramatically transformed after they witnessed the resurrection of Jesus. They became convinced that their brother was God in the flesh.

Good People Don't Die for a Lie They Know to Be False

Tradition tells us that after the resurrection, most of the twelve apostles were martyred, not just because of something they *said* believed in. They were martyred for something that they fervently believed to be true. People may die for a lie that they thought was true. But people do not die for a lie that they know to be false. Peter Kreeft, a philosophy professor at Boston College, says, "Why would the apostles lie? . . . If they lied, what was their motive, what did they get out of this? What they got out of it was misunderstanding, rejection, persecution, torture, and martyrdom. Hardly a list of perks."[22]

When I was a senior at Oak Hill Academy, I thought I would never attend a Christian university. But because I was young in the faith, I decided that I needed to grow. So I enrolled in a Christian university where I could grow in my knowledge of God and study the Scriptures. Liberty University holds chapel services three times a week. I didn't always pay attention in chapel, but I remember one particular meeting just before Easter break. Gary Habermas stood in front of thousands of students to present the historical evidence for the resurrection. After presenting a convincing argument for our faith in the bodily resurrection, he shared a personal story of how the resurrection of Jesus got him through one of the most difficult times in his own life. Habermas told us:

> I'll never forget the day after Easter, when I received the shocking news from my doctor, "Your wife has stomach cancer." That's arguably the worst kind of cancer you can get. So I called a close friend and asked him to take my four children out of school and tell them that their mother has stomach cancer. Weeks later, I sat on my porch as Debbie was sleeping. She had a tube coming out of her stomach, and I had to feed her through the tube three times a day. As Debbie slept, I sat on the porch and had my conversation with God, similar to that of Job in the Old Testament. I prayed, "Come on, God, she's only 43 years old, and she's up there dying. Lord, she is the mother of my children. She is my closest friend. Let her live."[23]

Even in the midst of his disappointment, Habermas knew that God shared his pain. "I felt like God had said, 'I know what you mean Gary, I understand your hurt,'" Habermas explained. "'I watched My Son die. I saw every whip lash. I watched Him asphyxiate. Do you expect better than My Son received? But Gary, I raised Him from the dead and I also will raise Debbie.'" Habermas continued:

> I tried to argue God out of it, and I didn't know that in just a few days I would hold my wife's hand for the very last time.

My wife was in a coma, and my sister-in-law, who is a nurse, put a stethoscope on her heart and told me to talk to her. So I told Debbie, "I love you, I love you, I love you." Debbie's sister told me that the most incredible thing happened. When I told Debbie that I loved her, her heart sped up. When I didn't say anything, her heart slowed down. A few minutes later, Debbie died. The date was April 9, 1995. I buried my best friend. Losing my wife was the most painful experience I've ever had to face, but if the Resurrection could help me get through her death, Christ's Resurrection can get us through anything. Heaven is living eternally with God and your loved ones. The resurrection of Jesus gives us assurance of heaven.

As I listened to Dr. Habermas' tender story, I decided to sign up for his theology course that summer. More importantly, I was encouraged by the simple words of Christ that Habermas reminded us of as he finished his sermon: "Because I live, you also will live."[24] Because Jesus rose from the dead, we also can have great hope for the future, even in the worst times of suffering and sorrow. Because of the resurrection, we can trust Jesus.

Chapter Nine

Why Should I Trust Jesus When I Have **Failed So Many Times?**

*"For though a righteous man
falls seven times, he rises again."*

—King Solomon (Proverbs 24:16)

If any of us were to put together a résumé of our life so far, trying our utmost to impress whoever was to read it, how many of our failures would we include? Most likely none. Failures are something we do our best to cover up when we're presenting ourselves to others. At the same time, we're sometimes tempted to focus on our failures rather than learn from them.

Sometimes failure is the result of a particular sin in our lives. Other times, failure has nothing to do with sin. In either case, our failures present another obstacle when it comes to trusting Jesus, especially when we feel we have failed many times. I have certainly failed many times in my life. As an athlete, I let my team down. As a writer, I have had manuscripts rejected by multiple publishers. As a student, I had to drop Latin. I've failed to raise financial support as a missionary. As a single man who has never married, I've failed in some of my dating relationships.

Have you ever felt like a failure? Maybe it was an unsuccessful career, a botched marriage, or a stupid mistake that ruined a friendship. Feeling like a complete failure can be a lonely experience. One mother expressed her feelings of failure to her pastor in this way:

I'm the world's number-one failure. My marriage is failing. I seem to do everything wrong in raising my children. I'm not very good at anything. I'm not even able to understand the Bible very well. Most of it is over my head. I feel as though I'm not worth anything to anyone. I've not been a very good wife, mother, or Christian. I have to be the world's greatest failure.[1]

One reason that I trust the Bible is that it does not hide the deficiencies of its heroes. In the Bible we see that:

- Abraham, the "friend of God," lied to save his skin.
- King David, the "man after God's heart," committed adultery with a good man's wife and then murdered him to cover up the evidence.
- Simon Peter, one of Jesus' three closest disciples, openly denied his Master three times, swearing that he "never knew the man."

Thankfully human failure is not the end of the story. In each of these cases, God showed His amazing grace, and these flawed human beings continued on to live productive lives of service to the Lord. In my own life, God has continued to bring success and favor despite my failures. Even though I was denied by publishers in the past, I've received multiple offers from publishing companies recently. The Lord has also provided an abundance of ministry opportunities, and my finances are coming back in order. Even though my last girlfriend broke up with me, I've grown as a godly man who will be ready to lead more wisely in my next relationship. Most importantly, I believe God has been drawing me closer to Him during the past year. If God can change me, there's hope for you!

If we submit ourselves to God with sincere humility, God will redeem our failures so that we can be better prepared for the Lord's service.

FAILURE IS NOT FATAL

History is full of the stories of men and women who failed but did not allow their failure to be fatal. Instead, they allowed their shortcomings to become opportunities for learning, improvement, and character growth. Consider these true accounts:

- In an effort to generate electric current, an aspiring inventor got two cats, attached a wire to their legs, and applied friction to their backs by rubbing them. The experiment was a great failure. The cats refused to cooperate and took to spitting and clawing before they ran off. The telegraph line had to be temporarily abandoned. However, the failure of this experiment did not discourage young Thomas Edison.[2]
- A writer thought his novel was worth publishing. He was rejected by twenty-eight agents and editors before finally finding a publisher for his first novel. And of his first printing of five thousand copies, he purchased one thousand himself and peddled them from the trunk of his car. John Grisham, however, was not derailed by failure. Today he is one of the most successful novelists, with more than sixty million books in print in thirty-one languages.[3]
- In a Nike TV commercial, a retired basketball player reflected back on his career:

  "I've missed 9,000 shots in my career . . .
  "I've lost almost 300 games . . .
  "26 times, I've been trusted to take the game-winning shot . . . and missed.
  "I've failed over and over again in my life . . ."
  But then, Michael Jordan added, ". . . and that is precisely why I succeed."[4]

Jordan, one of the greatest basketball players ever, did not allow his failures to be fatal.

No matter how many times you have failed, you can still trust Jesus. God is a God of great patience; He is quick to forgive and can enable you to add "another chapter" to your life story—a successful chapter.

HISTORY'S GREATEST FAILURE

The life of Abraham Lincoln ought to inspire anyone who has felt like a failure! Consider these events from his life:

- Difficult childhood
- Less than one year of formal schooling
- Failed in business in 1831
- Defeated for the legislature, 1832
- Again failed in business, 1833
- Elected to the legislature, 1834
- Fiancée died, 1835
- Defeated for Speaker, 1838
- Defeated for Elector, 1840
- Only one of his four sons lived past age 18
- Defeated for Congress, 1843
- Elected to Congress, 1846
- Defeated for Congress, 1848
- Defeated for Senate, 1855
- Defeated for Vice-President, 1856
- Defeated for Senate, 1858
- Elected President, 1860 [5]

You and I will make mistakes. But God, through His grace, will help us to become wiser in the future and to avoid making similar mistakes. No matter what we do, God gives us an opportunity to respond to the love of Jesus.

WHEN WE FAIL

Responding positively and wisely when we fail is one of the most important aspects of our character. We might call it *failing forward*. When things don't go our way, we always have the choice to pick ourselves up and press forward with renewed passion and faith. The following pointers can help you to keep your focus on trusting God even in the face of failure.

When we fail, we can appreciate the grace of God.

John Newton was remembered as a "foul-mouthed sailor whose wild behavior even shocked his less-than-perfect shipmates. He was a slave trader who had no conscience about buying and selling people for profit."[6] As Newton was sailing back to England from Africa in 1748, the slave ship *Greyhound* encountered a severe storm on the Atlantic triangle trade route and almost sank. As the ship filled with water in the middle of the night, Newton awoke and prayed to God to save his life. This terrifying experience was a real wake-up call for him. Newton eventually rejected the slave trade, became a minister, and later became instrumental in the abolition of slavery. Even though Newton had lived a life of many sins, he understood the grace of God.[7] After reflecting on his wretchedness, Newton penned the words to a famous hymn:

> Amazing grace, how sweet the sound,
> That saved a wretch like me.
> I once was lost but now am found,
> Was blind, but now I see.

Newton befriended and mentored the young politician William Wilberforce, who, after many years of persistence, helped to abolish slavery in the British Empire. Newton's final words are inspiring: "My memory is nearly gone, but I remember two things: that I am a great sinner, and that Christ is a great Savior."[8]

Another conversion account that gives hope to anyone who has ever failed God is that of the apostle Paul. Consider his testimony:

> Even though I was once a blasphemer and a persecutor and a violent man, I was shown mercy because I acted in ignorance and unbelief. The grace of our Lord was poured out on me abundantly, along with the faith and love that are in Christ Jesus. Here is a trustworthy saying that deserves full acceptance: Christ Jesus came into the world to save sinners— of whom I am the worst.[9]

You cannot do anything to make God love you less. Annie Johnson Flint put it this way:

> His love has no limit, His grace has no measure,
> His power no boundary known unto men;
> For out of his infinite riches in Jesus
> He giveth and giveth again.

There is no limit to Christ's grace and love. Even when you fail in your spiritual life or in any other aspect of life, He will forgive you and extend His infinite spiritual riches to you again.

When we fail, we can become better people.

After we fail, we can choose to learn from our experience and become better people. Jonas Salk, the great scientist who discovered the polio vaccine, understood the concept of remaining optimistic in the midst of failure. He was once asked, "How does this outstanding achievement, which has effectively brought an end to the word *polio* in our vocabulary, cause you to view your previous two hundred failures?"

His response (paraphrased) was, "I never had two hundred failures in my life. My family didn't think in terms of failure. They taught in terms of experiences and what could be learned. I just made my 20lst discovery. I couldn't have made it without learning from the previous two hundred experiences."[10]

An enterprising young man in Chicago started a cheese business. At first he failed miserably and was deeply in debt. A Christian friend challenged him. "You didn't take God into your business. You have not worked with Him."

That advice changed the young man's entire perspective. He thought, *If God wants to run the cheese business, He can do it, and I'll work for Him and with Him.* From that day on, God was the senior partner in his business, and the business prospered beyond his wildest imaginations. Perhaps you've heard of this young man: J. L. Kraft, founder of the largest cheese company in the world.[11]

Sometimes failures can be our greatest asset. We can become more careful, more sensitive, and more willing to trust God rather than ourselves. The apostle Paul wrote, "We do not want you to be uninformed, brothers, about the hardships we suffered in the province of Asia. We were under great pressure, far beyond our ability to endure, so that we despaired even of life. Indeed, in our hearts we felt the sentence of death. But this happened that we might not rely on ourselves but on God, who raises the dead."[12]

When we are weak, we clearly grasp our utter dependency on God. And when we are fully dependent on God, we finally see and understand how great He is, how small we are, and how much we desperately need Him.

When we fail, we can either give up or GET UP!

When I was in college, one of my pastor's favorite sermons dealt with failure. He would say, "When you are down, you have one of two choices: You can give up, or you can GET UP!" Give up or GET UP! Judas and Peter both faced these two options. Both men were disciples of Jesus. Both denied the Lord during His arrest and interrogation. But Judas gave in to despair and went out and hanged himself. Peter, on the other hand, responded to the Lord's grace, and received forgiveness and restoration.

Winston Churchill was another great man who was not intimidated by errors. When he made a mistake, he simply thought the problem through again. Someone asked him, "Sir Winston, what in your school experience best prepared you to lead Britain out of her darkest hour?" Churchill thought a minute and said, "It was the two years I spent at the same level in high school."

"Did you fail?" the person asked.

"No," replied Churchill. "I had two opportunities to get it right."[13]

When we fail, Scripture encourages us to GET UP! God doesn't see you as a failure. He understands that the Christian life is a process. He may simply be giving you one more opportunity to get it right. Proverbs 24:16 says, "For though a righteous man falls seven times, he rises again, but the wicked are brought down by calamity." Have you fallen lately? If so, don't stay down. Don't give up. Instead, get up and let God use you!

When we fail, we can receive God's greatest gift—His forgiveness.

Not all failures are caused by sin, but some certainly are. When we fail because of laziness, pride, lust, or greed, we must repent from our sinful and selfish ways and confess our sins to God. God promises us in Scripture that, "if we confess our sins, he is faithful and just and will forgive us our sins and purify us from all unrighteousness."[14]

The work of Christ on the cross was the perfect gift of forgiveness that cleanses all sins, no matter how bad they may seem. Paul, a former persecutor and murderer of Christians, realized the beauty of this gift of forgiveness when he encountered the love of Jesus. Later he wrote to a group of believers, "Thanks be to God for his indescribable gift!"[15] Peter, who denied Jesus three times, also grew to appreciate the priceless gift of God's forgiveness:

And God has reserved for his children the priceless gift of eternal life; it is kept in heaven for you, pure and undefiled, beyond reach of change and decay. And God, in his mighty power, will make sure that you get there safely to receive it, because you are trusting in him. It will be yours in that coming last day for all to see.[16]

God's sovereignty is so magnificent that He has given you and me free choice in accepting or rejecting this gift. God loves us enough to give us free will; He will not force us to trust in Him. True love cannot be compelled; we cannot love God if we do not have the option of rejecting Him. We must choose to receive the gift that God offers. Speaking of Jesus, John said, "Yet to all who received him, to those who believed in his name, he gave the right to become the children of God."[17]

We can be encouraged that our salvation from Christ does not depend on whether we feel like a success or a failure in life. The gift of God's salvation has nothing to do with what we have done. Imagine a needy child whose wealthy relative promises to give him an extraordinary gift. Would any child refuse such an incredible offer? Certainly not.

Through His death and resurrection, Christ offers us a free gift that will be far beyond anything we can imagine—abundant life right now and a life forever with God in heaven. God's extravagant package includes complete forgiveness of sins, inner joy, peace, contentment, a constant and loving companion in Christ, and the power of His Holy Spirit to help us live a consistent, God-pleasing life.

Maybe you have never opened this gift of grace. The gift is absolutely free; there is not a thing we can do to deserve it or earn it. As Max Lucado notes, Jesus holds out His nail-scarred hands and says to you, "I did it just for you."[18]

I want to heartily encourage you to trust in Jesus. I believe that this is the most important decision you will ever make in life. So, will you believe Him? Will you trust Him? If so, then join me in praying the following prayer, making this your personal faith declaration:

"Jesus Christ, I will trust in You. I will trust You because of who

You are, because You are fully God and fully human. I will trust You because of Your death and bodily resurrection. I will trust in Your salvation. Thank You for forgiving all of my sins. I will trust in Your lordship; please take over control of my life. I will trust You even though I have failed so many times. I will trust You when I do not fully understand. I will trust You in times of trouble. With Your help and because Your sovereignty has enabled me, I will trust in You, Jesus, all the days of my life. Amen."

Afterword

Why I Trust Jesus
JOSH McDOWELL

Dave Sterrett's book *Why Trust Jesus?* provides a true foundation of trust for both the Christian and the spiritual seeker. This book is very much needed in the church today. Dave tackles some of the toughest objections about trusting in Jesus in a way that is biblically true and relationally relevant.

When I was a teenager, I struggled with trust, just like a lot of people do today. This generation has been exposed to an assortment of deceptions that have implanted distrust deep in their hearts and minds. Hypocrisy, broken relationships, the moral decay of religious leaders, school shootings, terrorist attacks, and political dishonesty certainly have added to this problem.

In addition, our culture has embraced an individualistic, independent attitude toward life. Many people don't see the need to trust anybody. They are confident that they can achieve the good life on their own apart from others. But I'm convinced that God has created us as relational people. As Dave writes, "This generation isn't necessarily opposed to spirituality or Jesus Himself, but is perhaps like I was—longing for authentic, fulfilling relationships and true freedom." This new book on Christ gives us confidence that Jesus is trustworthy, even when life isn't working out like we thought it would.

When I was a teenager, I wanted to be free to trust, but I felt like couldn't. So I started looking for answers—something or someone whom I could *trust*. It seemed that almost everyone I knew was into some sort of religion, so I did the obvious thing and went to church. I must have visited the wrong church, though, because it only made me feel worse. I went to church morning, noon, and night, but it didn't help. I'm very practical, and when something doesn't work, I chuck it. So I gave up on religion.

I began to wonder if I could find something trustworthy in education, so I enrolled in the university. What a disappointment! You can find a lot of things at a university, but enrolling there to find spiritual truth and meaning in life is virtually a lost cause. I soon realized that the university didn't have the answers I was seeking. Faculty members and my fellow students had just as many problems, frustrations, and unanswered questions about life as I did. Education was not what I was looking for.

During that time I noticed a small group of people—eight students and two faculty members. There was something different about their lives. They seemed to know why they believed what they believed. They didn't just *talk* about love, they got involved in people's lives. They seemed to be riding above the circumstances of university life. They had something I didn't have.

As my relationship with this group continued, they challenged me over and over to examine the evidence of Christianity. Finally,

I accepted their challenge. I did it out of pride to refute them, thinking there were no facts. I assumed there wasn't any real evidence for me to evaluate. However, through months of intensive study, I discovered that Jesus Christ must have been who He claimed to be. That presented quite a problem for me. My mind told me all this was true, but my will was pulling me in another direction.

I came to the point where I'd go to bed at ten at night, and I wouldn't fall asleep until four in the morning. I knew I had to get this issue off my mind before I went crazy! Finally, my head and my heart connected on December 19, 1959, at 8:30 p.m., during my second year at the university. I placed my trust in Jesus.

I'm sure you've heard various religious people talking about their personal bolt-of-lightning experience. Well, you won't hear that from me. After I prayed, nothing happened. I mean nothing. I didn't sprout angel wings. In fact, after I made my decision, I felt worse. *Oh, no*, I thought, *what did you get sucked into now?* I really felt I'd gone off the deep end (and I'm sure some people think I did!).

But after about a year, I found out that I hadn't gone off the deep end. My life *was* changed. Let me tell you one area in which my trust was changed. It's in an area of which I'm not proud. There was one man that I distrusted more than anyone else in the world: my father. I hated his guts. To me, he was the town alcoholic. Everybody knew my dad was a drunk. My friends would make jokes about my father staggering around downtown. They didn't think it bothered me. Like other people, I was laughing on the outside. But let me tell you, I was crying on the inside. There were times I'd go out in the barn and see my mother beaten so badly she couldn't get up, lying in the manure behind the cows.

When we had friends over, I would take my father out, tie him up in the barn, and park the car around the silo. We would tell our friends he'd had to go somewhere. I don't think anyone could have hated anyone more than I hated my father. But after I made my decision for Christ, Jesus entered my life. His love was so strong that He took the hatred and turned it upside down. I was able to look my father squarely in the eyes and say, "Dad, I love you." And I really meant it. After some of the things I'd done, that shook him up.

After I transferred to a private university, I was in a serious car accident. I was taken home with my neck in traction. I'll never forget my father coming into my room. He asked me, "Son, how can you love a father like me?"

I said, "Dad, six months ago I despised you." Then I shared with him the conclusions I had come to about Christ: "I let Jesus Christ come into my life. I can't explain it completely, but as a result of that relationship, I've found the capacity to love and accept not only you but other people just the way they are."

Forty-five minutes later, one of the greatest thrills of my life occurred. Somebody in my own family, someone who knew me so well I couldn't pull the wool over his eyes, said to me, "Son, if God can do in my life what I've seen Him do in yours, then I want to give Him the opportunity." Right there, my father prayed with me and trusted Christ for the forgiveness of his sins.

Usually, changes in a person's life take place over several days, weeks, months, or even a year. But my father's life was changed right before my eyes. It was as if somebody reached down and turned on a light. I've never seen such a rapid change before or since. My father touched whiskey only once after that. He got it as far as his lips, and that was it. He couldn't take a drink.

I've come to one conclusion: a relationship with Jesus Christ changes lives. You can laugh at Christianity. You can mock and ridicule it. But it changes lives. As you have read Dave's book and heard my testimony, I pray that you will open up your heart and experience trusting in Jesus.

Acknowledgments

Thank you Dad and Mom for reading the entire book and for providing helpful suggestions. Your encouragement, biblical wisdom, and practical advice are a blessing.

Thank you Josh McDowell and Bryan Davidson for believing in the idea of this book, years ago, when I was in my early twenties and just getting starting with sharing the message of "Why Trust Jesus?" in churches and schools.

Marla Alupoaicei, you did an excellent job reviewing the book. Your literary services are very much appreciated.

Thank you Norman Geisler, Frank Turek, Jonathan Merritt, Jack Graham, Gary Habermas, David McKinley, Ethan Pope, Curt and Karol Ladd, Becki Stevenson, Erica Wall, Caroline Lewis, Bill Sterrett, Shay Todd, Ward Coleman, Timothy "Tag" Green, O.S. Hawkins, Gerald Brooks, Dan Panetti, Craig Foster, Katie Newlen, Becky Newlen, Bryce Taylor, Ergun Caner, Ed Hindson, Zig Ziglar, Kerby Anderson, Elmer Towns, and Adrienne Carpenter for reading portions of the initial manuscript and for providing encouragement, prayers, coaching, or needed corrections. Your faith and friendship, through God's Spirit, motivated me to complete this project.

Thank you Katherine Robertson for being my photographer for promotional material.

Thank you Randall Payleitner, my acquisitions editor, Brandon O'Brien, my editor, and Pam Pugh, the general project editor of Moody, for making this book a reality.

Notes

Introduction: The Need for Transparent Trust

1. Psalm 27:13 (NASB)
2. Unless otherwise indicated, names have been changed for privacy.
3. Liza Porteus, "Federal Official: At Least 32 Dead after Virginia Tech Shooting," *FoxNews.com*, www.foxnews.com/story/0,2933,266310,00.html.
4. Luke 23:4 (KJV)
5. Deuteronomy 32:4 (NASB)

Chapter One:
Why Should I Trust Jesus When There Are So Many Other Spiritual Paths?

1. Acts 4:12
2. John 14:6
3. Ravi Zacharias, *Jesus Among Other Gods* (Nashville: W Publishing Group, 2000), vii.
4. Ibid.
5. Oprah Winfrey as quoted in video clip posted on multiple sites, including http://www.jesus-is-savior.com/Wolves/oprah-fool.htm For more information, see Dave Sterrett's coauthored book *"O" God: A Dialogue on Truth and Oprah's Spirituality* (Los Angeles: WNDBooks, 2009).
6. Ibid.
7. Britney Spears quote found on multiple sites, including http://www.celebs quotes.com/b/britney-spears/
8. J. P. Moreland, *Kingdom Triangle* (Grand Rapids: Zondervan, 2007), 12.
9. John 14:1–7
10. John 14:8, 11
11. Paul Copan, *True for You, But Not for Me* (Minneapolis: Bethany House Publishers, 1998), 18.
12. Ibid.
13. R. C. Sproul, *Discovering the God Who Is* (Ventura: Regal, 2007), 178.
14. This quote is found on multiple Internet sites, including the article "How Mandy Deals with Life," which can be found on http://encarta.msn.com/encnet/departments/college/?article=MandyMoore.

15. Josh McDowell and Bob Hostetler, *Beyond Belief to Convictions* (Wheaton: Tyndale House Publishers, 2002), 7.

16. Matthew 22:37

17. Isaiah 1:18

18. Matthew 16:24

19. 1 Timothy 4:7 (NASB)

20. Psalm 9:10

21. Jeremiah 29:13 (NASB)

22. Psalm 20:7

Chapter Two:
Why Should I Trust Jesus When I'm not Sure That a Supernatural God Is Real?

1. Lucretius quote found on multiple sites, including the C. S. Lewis Institute, http://www.cslewisinstitute.org/cslewis/mostReluctantConvertBR.htm.

2. C. S. Lewis, *Surprised by Joy* (New York: A Harvest Book, 1955), 228.

3. Acts 17

4. St. Augustine, *On Christian Teaching* 4.4. (Oxford: Oxford University Press, 1997).

5. Lewis, *Learning in War-Time*, In: *The Weight of Glory* (New York: Macmillan Publishing Company, 1980), 28.

6. *Expelled: The Movie.* Directed by Ben Stein: Premise Media Corporation, 2008.

7. *Contact.* Directed by Robert Zemeckis: Hollywood, CA: Warner Brothers USA, 1997, illustration used by Alex McFarland, *The 10 Most Common Objections to Christianity* (Ventura: Regal Books, 2007), 44.

8. William Paley, *The Works of William Paley,* vol. 4,1 (Oxford: Claredon Press, 1938). Quoted by Dinesh D'Souza, *What's So Great about Christianity* (Washington: Regnery Publishing, 2007), 139.

9. Ibid.

10. *Reasons to Believe,* http://www.reasons.org, hosted by Dr. Hugh Ross.

11. Francis S. Collins, *The Language of God* (New York: Free Press, 2006), taken from author biography on back cover.

12. Ibid., 2.

13. Ibid.

14. David Hume, in J. Y. T. Greig, ed., *The Letters of David Hume* (New York: Garland, 1983), 1:1187. Quoted by Norman L. Geisler and Frank Turek, *I Don't Have Enough Faith to Be an Atheist* (Wheaton: Crossway Books, 2004), 75.

15. Ibid.

16. Stephen Hawking and Roger Penrose, *The Nature of Space and Time*, The Isaac Newton Institute Series of Lectures (Princeton, NJ: Princeton Univer-

sity Press, 1996), 20. Quoted by Chad Meister, *Building Belief* (Grand Rapids: Baker Books, 2006), 97.

17. G. L. Schroeder, *The Science of God* (New York: Broadway Books, 1997), 138.

18. Robert Jastrow, *God and the Astronomers* (Toronto: Readers Library, 1992), 14.

19. Plato, *Theaetetus* 152A3 (indianapolis: Hackett Publishing 1997).

20. C. S. Lewis, *Mere Christianity* (New York: HarperCollins Edition, 2001), 6.

21. Dr. Martin Luther King Jr. recorded on multiple sources, including http://www.stanford.edu/group/King/publications.

22. Romans 7:14–15 (HCSB)

23. Romans 7:21–24 (HCSB)

24. Romans 7:24–25 (NLT)

Chapter 3:
Why Should I Trust Jesus When I Have Been Let Down So Many Times?

1. J. B. Phillips, *Your God Is Too Small* (New York: Touchstone, 1952), 48.

2. Romans 8:31

3. Hebrews 13:5

4. Philippians 4:12–13 (NLT)

5. John 6:14–15 (HCSB)

6. John 6:53–55 (ESV)

7. John 6: 60–61, 66 (HCSB)

8. Elizabeth Gilbert, *Eat, Pray, Love* (New York: Penguin, 2007), 53.

9. John 6:67–69 (HCSB)

10. Matthew 11:3 (HCSB)

11. Matthew 11:4–5 (HCSB)

12. Psalm 27:13 (NASB)

13. Romans 8:28

14. Norman L. Geisler, *Baker Encyclopedia of Christian Apologetics* (Grand Rapids: Baker, 1999), 221.

15. William Lane Craig, *Hard Questions, Real Answers* (Wheaton: Crossway, 2003), 80–81.

16. John 16:33

17. 2 Corinthians 4:17–18 (NLT)

18. Romans 8:18 (NKJV)

19. Revelation 21:1–4 (NLT)

20. Paraphrased from Daniel 1

21. Daniel 3:1–6, paraphrased.

22. Daniel 3:16–18 (NLT)

23. James 1:2–4

24. Psalm 13:1–2

25. Psalm 13:5–6

26. C. S. Lewis, *The Screwtape Letters* (New York: HarperCollins Edition, 2001), 40.

Chapter Four:
Why Should I Trust Jesus When Life Seems to Be Going Just Fine without Him?

1. Augustine, *Confessions* 1.5

2. Ibid., 1.1.1.

3. Ibid., 3.11

4. Ibid., 2.3

5. Ibid., 8.7.17

6. Romans 13:14 (KJV)

7. 1 Peter 2:11

8. Romans 4:4–5

9. Augustine, *Confessions* 1.

10. Matthew 11:28–29

11. 1 Kings 4:29

12. Eugene Peterson, *The Message* (Colorado: NavPress, 2002), 882.

13. Ecclesiastes 2:1–10 (THE MESSAGE)

14. Ecclesiastes 2:11 (THE MESSAGE)

15. See 1 Timothy 6:17–19

16. Proverbs 14:12

17. 1 Timothy 6:10

18. 1 Timothy 6:17

19. Inspired and adapted from Rob Bell's *Nooma* video called *Rich*.

20. Deuteronomy 8:17–18

21. Psalm 42:1–2

22. Isaiah 55:6

23. 2 Corinthians 4:18

24. Mark 8:36

25. John 10:10 (NKJV)

26. Ecclesiasties 2:24 (NKJV)

27. Psalm 16:11

28. Hebrews 11:24–26 (NLT)

29. C. S. Lewis, *The Weight of Glory and Other Essays* (Grand Rapids: Eerdmans, 1965), 1–2.

30. 1 Peter 1:8

31. John 10:10

32. Philippians 4:6–7

33. Luke 16:11

34. Psalm 16:11

35. 1 Timothy 6:19 (NLT)

Chapter Five:
Why Should I Trust Jesus When All I Need to Do Is Trust Myself?

1. Deepak Chopra, *The Third Jesus* (New York: Harmony, 2008), 212.

2. Geisler, *Baker Encyclopedia of Christian Apologetics* (Grand Rapids: Baker, 1998), 580.

3. Ted Cabal, "How Should a Christian Relate to the New Age Movement?", *The Apologetics Study Bible*, 1784 (Nashville: Holman Bible Publishers), 2007.

4. Geisler, *Baker Encyclopedia of Christian Apologetics*, 581.

5. Marianne Williamson, *A Course in Miracles*, lesson 1, found on *Oprah and Friends Radio*, posted on http://www2.oprah.com/xm/mwilliamson/200801/mwilliamson_20080101.jhtml.

6. Ibid, lesson 70.

7. Dan Brown, *The Lost Symbol* (New York: Doubleday, 2009), 58.

8. Helen Schucman, *A Course in Miracles*, published by A Foundation of Inner Peace, found on http://www.acim.org/index.html.

9. Ibid.

10. Geisler, *Baker Encyclopedia of Christian Apologetics*, 581.

11. Psalm 51:5; Romans 3:23; Ephesians 2:3

12. John 4:24

13. A. W. Tozer, *Knowledge of the Holy* (San Francisco: Harper Collins, 1961), 1.

14. R. C. Sproul, *Now That's a Good Question!* (Wheaton: Tyndale Publishers, 1996), 14. Quoted by Alex McFarland, *The 10 Most Common Objections to Christianity* (Ventura: Regal Books, 2007), 22.

15. John 4:10 (HCSB)

16. John 4:11–14 (HCSB)

17. Psalm 113:4–6

18. Isaiah 55:8–9

19. John 7:37

20. Isaiah 55:1 (NLT)

21. Revelation 22:17

22. John 4:39
23. John 1:48–51 (HCSB)
24. Proverbs 15:3
25. Job 37:16
26. Psalm 147:5 (AMP)
27. See Matthew 10:30
28. Colossians 2:3 (NASB)
29. Romans 8:28 (HCSB)
30. Colossians 1:15–17 (HCSB)
31. Ephesians 2:10 (The Jerusalem Bible)
32. Ephesians 2:10 (NLT)
33. Psalm 139:13–14 (HCSB)
34. Malachi 3:6
35. 2 Timothy 2:13
36. Hebrews 13:8
37. Geisler, *Baker Encyclopedia of Christian Apologetics,* 581.

Chapter Six:
Why Should I Trust Jesus When There Is So Much Disagreement about the Identity of the "Real Jesus"?

1. Mark Driscoll and Gerry Breshears, *Vintage Jesus* (Wheaton: Crossway Books, 2007), 13.
2. *Rock N Roll Jesus* by Kid Rock. Detroit: RJR Publishing, Jo Ray Dean Music (BMI), Bulldog Detroit (BMI), 1997.
3. John Lennon cited by Franklin Graham, *The Name* (Nashville: Thomas Nelson, 2002), 3.
4. Bertrand Russell, *Why I Am Not a Christian* (New York: Simon Schuster, 1957), 16.
5. Franklin Graham, *The Name*, 3.
6. Ibid.
7. Josh McDowell, *More Than a Carpenter* (Wheaton: Tyndale House Publishers, 1977), 7.
8. Gnosticism summary was adapted from Norman L. Geisler, *Baker Encyclopedia of Christian Apologetics* (Grand Rapids: Baker, 1998), 273.
9. Thomas 7 in *Lost Scriptures: Books That Did Not Make the New Testament,* ed. Bart D. Ehrman (Oxford: Oxford University Press, 2003), 20.
10. Ibid.
11. John Warwick Montgomery, "Could the Gospel Writers Withstand the Scrutiny of a Lawyer?" in *The Apologetics Study Bible*, ed. Ted Cabal (Nashville: Holman Bible Publishers, 2007), 1511.

12. Flavius Josephus quoted by Norman L. Geisler and Frank Turek, *I Don't Have Enough Faith to Be an Atheist* (Wheaton: Crossway Books, 2004), 221.

13. Wilkins, Jesus Under Fire, 222 quoted by Josh McDowell, *New Evidence That Demands a Verdict* (Nashville: Thomas Nelson, 1999), 60.

14. Norman L. Geisler and Frank Turek, *I Don't Have Enough Faith to Be an Atheist* (Wheaton: Crossway Books, 2004), 222.

15. Luke 1:1–4

16. 2 Peter 1:16

17. 1 John 1:1–2

18. Acts 2:32

19. 1 Corinthians 15:6

20. Josh McDowell and Bob Hostetler, *Beyond Belief to Convictions* (Wheaton: Tyndale, 2002), 63.

21. Ibid.

22. Isaiah 53:2–12

23. Lee Strobel, *The Case for the Real Jesus* (Grand Rapids: Zondervan, 2007), 212.

24. Ibid.

Chapter 7:
Why Should I Trust Jesus More Than Any Other Spiritual Leader?

1. John 15:20

2. Matthew 10: 38–39 (HCSB)

3. John 1:29 (NKJV)

4. John 10:18

5. Acts 2:23 (NLT)

6. John 18:38; 19:6

7. Romans 5:7–8

8. John 14:6

9. John 8:49

10. Matthew 11:19

11. Dan Brown, *The DaVinci Code* (New York: Doubleday, 2003).

12. *The Da Vinci Code* rebuttal and deity quotes adapted from Lee Strobel and Gary Poole, *Exploring the Da Vinci Code* (Grand Rapids: Zondervan, 2006), 90.

13. Matthew 16:16

14. John 20:28

15. Colossians 2:9

16. Hebrews 1:8

17. Ignatius quoted by Lee Strobel and Gary Poole, *Exploring the Da Vinci Code* (Grand Rapids: Zondervan, 2006), 90.

18. Clement quoted by Lee Strobel and Gary Poole, *Exploring the DaVinci Code* (Grand Rapids: Zondervan, 2006), 90.

19. Exodus 3:14

20. John 8:52–59

21. Mark 2:7

22. John 5:18

23. For example, God calls the prophet Ezekiel on several occasions "son of man" (Ezekiel 2:1; 3:1; etc.).

24. Matthew 4:10

25. Daniel 7:13–14

26. Mark 14:61–62

27. Mark 14:63–65

28. Timothy Keller, *The Reason for God* (New York: Dutton, 2008), 229.

29. Mark Driscoll and Gary Breshears, *Vintage Jesus* (Wheaton: Crossway Books, 2007), 31.

30. Mark 5:30

31. Philippians 2:6–8

32. Philippians 2:9–11

33. Philip Schaff, *The Person of Christ*, 29–30, unpublished class notes from Dr. Leventhal in New Testament Survey at Southern Evangelical Seminary.

34. John 19:28

35. Max Lucado, *He Chose the Nails* (Nashville: Thomas Nelson, 2000), 92.

36. Hebrews 4:15

37. Luke 2:48

38. Isaiah 53:3

39. Matthew 27:46

40. Hebrews 2:17–18 (NKJV)

Chapter Eight:
Why Should I Trust Jesus in the Midst of Suffering and Death?

1. Introduction and reference to Maier's novel adapted from the introduction of Dillon Burrough, *The Jesus Family Tomb Controversy: How the Evidence Falls Short* (Ann Arbor: Nimble Books, 2007).

2. Hebrews 11:6

3. 1 Corinthians 15:17–19 (HCSB)

4. John 14:19

5. Naomi Wolf, *The Beauty Myth* (Toronto: Random House, 1990), 94.

6. 1 Corinthians 6:19–20

7. John 5:28–29

8. Hebrews 2:14–15; 1 Corinthians 15:20–58

9. 1 Peter 1:3–4

10. This is the only point that does not meet the criteria of "minimum facts." Nevertheless, Habermas reports that nearly 75 percent of scholars on the subject accept the empty tomb as a historical fact.

11. Gary Habermas, *Risen Jesus and Future Hope*, 9–10. Quoted by Geisler and Turek, *I Don't Have Enough Faith to Be an Atheist*, 299–300.

12. Hank Hanegraaff, *Resurrection* (Nashville: Word Publishing, 2000), 15.

13. Ibid.

14. Gary R. Habermas and Michael R. Licona, *The Case for the Resurrection*, (Grand Rapids, Kregel, 2004), 49.

15. Edwards, MD; Wesley J. Gabel, MDiv; Floyd E. Hosmer, MS, AMI *Journal of the American Medical Association*. 1986; 255(11):1455.

16. Edited by Paul Copan and Ronald K. Tacelli, *Jesus' Resurrection: Fact or Figment? A Debate between William Lane Craig and Gerd Ludemann* (Downers Grove, IL: InterVarsity Press), 10.

17. Ibid., 28.

18. 1 Corinthians 15:1–8 (HCSB)

19. William Lane Craig, "Did Jesus Really Rise from the Dead?", *Apologetics Study Bible* (Nashville: B&H Publishing, 2007), 1728.

20. Lee Strobel, *The Case for Christ*, 310.

21. Acts 2:22–40 (HCSB)

22. Geisler and Turek, *I Don't Have Enough Faith to Be an Atheist*, 275.

23. Dr. Habermas's testimony adapted from several podcast testimonies on www.garyhabermas.com.

24. John 14:19

Chapter Nine:
Why Should I Trust Jesus When I Have Failed So Many Times?

1. Letter written to David Wilkerson, cited in *Have You Felt Like Giving Up Lately?* (Old Tappan, NJ: Fleming H. Revell Co., 1980), 115.

2. Margaret Cousins, *The Story of Thomas Alva Edison* (New York: Landmark Books, 1981), 22.

3. Adapted from Larry Tomcak, *Reckless Abandon* (Lake Mary, FL: Charisma House, 2002), 207.

4. Michael Jordan, "Failure" Nike commercial.

5. John Maxwell, *Your Attitude: Key to Success* (San Bernardino, CA: Here's Life Publishers, 1984), 80.

6. Adapted from www.amazinggrace.ie/story_6.html.

7. Adapted from www.wikipedia.com.

8. Adapted from www.amazinggrace.ie/story_6.html.

9. 1 Timothy 1:13–15

10. H. Stephen Glenn and Jane Nelsen, *Raising Self-Reliant Children in a Self-Indulgent World* (Rocklin, CA: Prima Publishing and Communication, 1989), 73.

11. Francis Anfuso, article in *People of Destiny Magazine* (Gaithersburg, MD) Nov./Dec. 1988 issue.

12. 2 Corinthians 1:8–9

13. John Ortberg, *If You Want to Walk on Water, You've Got to Get Out of the Boat* (Grand Rapids: Zondervan, 2001), 23.

14. 1 John 1:9

15. 2 Corinthians 9:15

16. 1 Peter 1:4–5 (TLB)

17. John 1:12

18. Max Lucado, *He Chose the Nails* (Nashville: W Publishing Group, 2000), 27.